RAILWAYS OF BUCHAN

KEITH FENWICK AND DOUGLAS FLETT

Published by

THE GREAT NORTH OF SCOTLAND RAILWAY ASSOCIATION

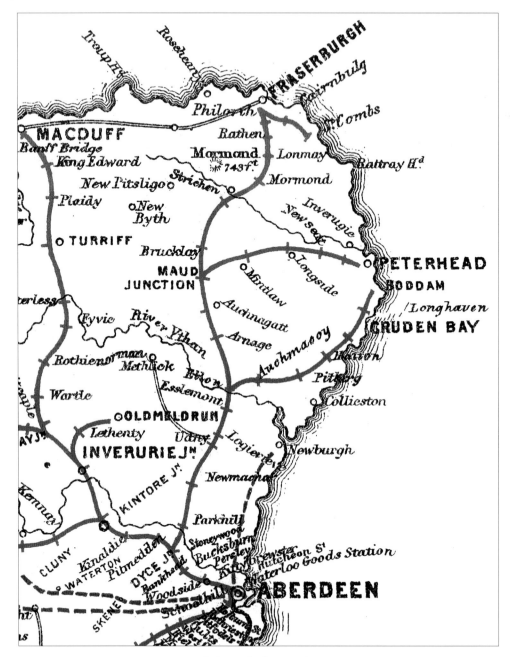

Acknowledgements

Grateful thanks go to various members of the Great North of Scotland Railway Association for their assistance in the preparation of this book. Photographs taken by Sandy Murdoch and Norris Forrest and from the GNSRA collection. OS maps are reproduced by courtesy of the Trustees of the National Library of Scotland.

Cover photo: A busy few minutes at Maud as passengers transfer from the Peterhead train on the right to the connecting service from Fraserburgh to Aberdeen on the left. A volume of parcels traffic has also to be transferred. The locomotives are D6138 and D6141.   (Graham Maxtone collection)

Contents

Published by the Great North of Scotland Railway Association

Printed by Henry Ling Limited at the Dorset Press, Dorchester, DT1 1HD

ISBN 978 0 902343 34 4

The raised ground on the west side of Maud station gave a grand view of the activities there and was a favourite place for photographers over the years. This view was taken in the early 1950s and shows an ex-North British Railway J36 0-6-0 shunting cattle wagons. Beyond the sidings, the Fraserburgh platform can be seen in the middle and the Peterhead ones in the distance. (Sandy Murdoch)

INTRODUCTION

Formartine and Buchan, two of the ancient Scottish provinces, form the north-east shoulder of Scotland. Characterised by rolling countryside, never very high but with many ridges and hollows, it is always exposed to the wind. After centuries of hard work the area now contains some of the best agricultural land in Scotland and is renowned in particular for producing fine beef cattle. At one time it was said that the farmsteads could be seen from a distance as they often had trees planted for shelter but since the end of the First World War there has also been a considerable increase in the amount of woodland, particularly on the poorer ground to the north, which has helped to soften the former rather bleak appearance.

Near Strichen lies Mormond Hill, 769 feet high, the highest point in Buchan. The hill itself has two well known landmarks – a horse on the south-west slope and a deer on the south-east. Sadly the summit ridge is now defaced by an array of telecoms equipment.

Small harbours around the coast are mainly used for recreation but they are overshadowed by the large fishing ports at Fraserburgh and Peterhead. Even today despite restrictions to conserve stocks,

fishing still plays a big part in the local economy while at Peterhead the oil industry in the North Sea has had a major impact.

Buchan was not easy country for the railway builders since any route running north from Aberdeen had to cross the valleys of the Don and Ythan. Beyond the River Ythan the terrain became somewhat easier but the engineers were still faced with frequent rises and falls resulting from earlier glaciation. Moreover, settlements were well dispersed over the area, so whichever route was chosen would favour some over others.

This book first appeared in 2008 in smaller format. This enlarged edition includes the text and many photographs from the original edition with several new illustrations. Changes in recent years are described, including the development of the interesting railway museum at Maud.

View from the cab of a train near Longside, where a house had to be trimmed to let the line pass by. This is similar to the better known example at Cambus o'May

Characteristic Buchan countryside is crossed by this D41 hauled freight near Brucklay in 1950. Covered wagons were used for fish traffic and general merchandise.   (Sandy Murdoch)

Before the Railways - these extracts from the *Aberdeen Directory* give a sample of services which were available in the earlier part of the 19th century.

A Coach to Peterhead, 1824-25.
With the mail leaves Dempster's Royal Mail Coach Office, 63 Union Street, or Anderson's Royal Mail Coach Office, 5 Castle Street, every day at 4 o'clock pm. Sets out from Peterhead next morning at half past 10 and arrives at Aberdeen at 3pm. Carries 4 inside and 4 outside passengers.

Ellon, Old Deer and Strichen, 1850-51
"Banks of Ythan" starts from Dean's Inn, Queen Street, for Ellon every lawful day at 3pm, to Strichen every Monday and Friday and to Old Deer every Wednesday and Saturday.

The Earl of Errol Coach
Sets out from Gray's, 18 Frederick Street every day (Sunday excepted) at 3 o'clock pm and arrives Jaffrey's Inn, Peterhead at 8pm. Leaves said Inn at 6am and reaches Aberdeen at 11am. Carries 4 inside and 8 outside passengers. Fare to Ellon 5/-, outside 4/-. Peterhead 10/-, outside 8/-.

EARLY SCHEMES AND CONTESTS

When the Great North of Scotland Railway was promoted at the height of the railway mania in 1845, it was for a main line from Aberdeen to Inverness along with several branches, none of which served Buchan. Its promoters, mainly Aberdeen business and legal men, were also behind the Aberdeen Railway from Forfar which completed the chain of lines from Carlisle, Edinburgh and Glasgow to the granite city. The Aberdeen Railway opened to Ferryhill in 1850 and was completed to the centre of the city in 1854 by which time its directorship had split from the Great North. It was 1867 before a new Joint Station serving routes to both north and south of Aberdeen was created on an adjacent site.

Back in 1845, the promoters of the GNSR could not afford to ignore the rich countryside on either side of its route. Among several other schemes put forward was the Great North of Scotland (Eastern Extension) Railway which was to run from Dyce via Ellon, Stuartfield, Old Deer and Mintlaw to Fraserburgh with a branch from Stuartfield to Peterhead. The estimated cost was £400,000. The GNSR main line and the Eastern Extension were both authorised in 1846, but by then it was impossible to raise the necessary funds to begin construction. The Eastern Extension was abandoned and the company wound up but the Great North itself persevered and eventually opened the first part of its line, from Kittybrewster to Huntly, in 1854.

During the previous year, the other railway from Aberdeen which had been proposed during the 1840s came to fruition when the Deeside Railway to Banchory was opened; its management was completely separate from that of the GNSR.

The opening of the Great North sparked a renewed interest in railway construction so it is not surprising that attention turned to the Buchan area. Late in 1853, the engineer to the Deeside Railway surveyed a line from Kittybrewster via Ellon, Arnage and Mintlaw to Peterhead; a branch to Strichen was also put forward, leaving Fraserburgh out. The Great North refused to give financial support to this line, on the grounds that its resources were only to be devoted to its main line. This led to the proposal, very much driven by John Duncan, chairman of the Deeside, for a line completely independent of the GNSR. The Aberdeen, Peterhead & Fraserburgh Railway was promoted in the autumn of 1855 to run from Aberdeen via Logierieve, Ellon and Mintlaw to Peterhead with branches from Mintlaw to Fraserburgh, Logierieve to Newburgh and New Leeds to Strichen.

The Great North now had to look more favourably on branch lines as it could not let a rival tap the rich territory of Buchan. It dusted down the 1846 plans and promoted the line as the Formartine & Buchan Railway. Fraserburgh was to be served by a branch from Maud which went west of Mormond Hill. House of Commons examination of the two Bills occupied several days during June 1856. The F&B Bill was rejected, but that of the AP&F approved on the casting vote of the committee chairman, leading to much rejoicing in the Buchan area but an upsurge in opposition at Aberdeen. The AP&F Bill still had to pass the House of Lords Committee, which considered it in July but discovered that some of the share subscriptions were not *bona fide*.

That was the end of the AP&F for that session but John Duncan quickly got back on the road to ensure continuing support for his line. Later in July, he was addressing

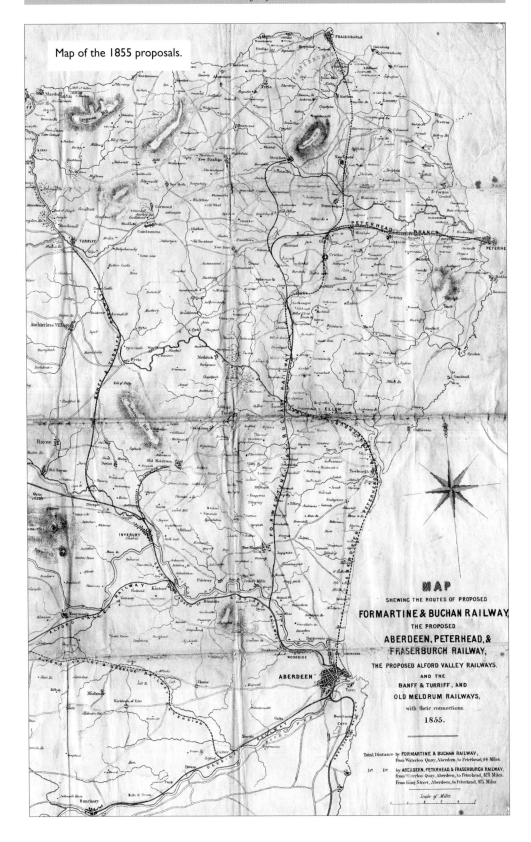

Map of the 1855 proposals.

several meetings in the district. Rival meetings were also held by the supporters of the F&B which relied in part on serving areas omitted by the AP&F.

The AP&F was planned to leave Aberdeen by a coastal route, conveniently serving Newburgh, but cutting across the Links and this led to strong opposition in Aberdeen itself. Public meetings were called and resolutions passed. Further north the line did not take a direct route to Peterhead but rather diverted inland to serve Ellon and then followed largely the route of the F&B.

MY LORD PROVOST,—I am instructed by the Committee of the Inhabitants for co-operating with the Town Council in the defence of the Links, to acquaint you, and the Council, that the signing of the Petition to the House of Lords against the threatened encroachment on the Links, which the Committee put in circulation, is all but completed. I am also directed to state, for your information, that the sheets have been most carefully gone over and scrutinised by a Sub-Committee of our number; and that the Petition is ascertained to be signed by upwards of *Eight Thousand* of our townsmen, all of whom append their designations.

It will thus be evident to the Council that the Petition expresses the settled convictions of a very large majority of the community, and the Committee believe that it will be felt by your Lordship and the Council as a conclusive proof of the warm sympathy with which the constituency view the firm and consistent course of conduct throughout pursued by you on this subject, and as an encouragement (if you need any) to persevere in it.

I have again to assure you of every aid and support which this Committee can give you, either here or in the House of Lords.

I have the honour to be, my Lord Provost, very respectfully, your most obedient servant,

J. URQUHART,
Chairman of the General Committee
of the Inhabitants for the defence of
the Links.

Sir Thomas Blaikie,
Lord Provost of Aberdeen.

With public support and opposition for both schemes, Bills were submitted again in November 1856. The *Railway Times* commented that the contest between these two parties had been one of the marvels of the 1856 session. Now it was to be renewed in the 1857 session but with little increased support for either scheme from the people of the district. As a result, the GNSR increased its subscription from £15,000 to £50,000. However, both of these Bills failed to comply with Standing Orders, so another year's delay ensued.

Meantime the Formartine & Buchan promoters had a new survey made and since this line would lie west of Ellon, a short branch to that town was included. Further north, there would be a junction at Mintlaw with the two branches following much the same routes to Peterhead and Fraserburgh as the AP&F. The promoters argued that, by running further inland and having its junction with the Great North and hence the rest of the railway system at Dyce, it would better serve the countryside than one following the coast and having no direct connection to other railways.

For the third time, notice of intention to submit the Bills was given in November 1857 and both came before the Commons Committee in the following May. After five days of examination of witnesses, the AP&F Bill was rejected but the F&B approved. The latter then went forward to the Lords Committee, which only took two days to approve the Bill, although on the second day it had to move to a different room because of the stench from the River Thames. All these deliberations were reported in detail by the Aberdeen newspapers, such was the interest in the schemes.

At the end of the day, the attempt by John Duncan to create a credible rival to the GNSR was defeated and it was left to the latter to push forward the lines to Fraserburgh and Peterhead. It was to take another seven years before both termini were reached.

ANNO VICESIMO PRIMO & VICESIMO SECUNDO

VICTORIÆ REGINÆ.

****

Cap. cviii.

An Act for making a Railway from the *Great North
of Scotland* Railway to *Old Deer*, and thence to
Peterhead and *Fraserburgh*, with a Branch to
Ellon, all in the County of *Aberdeen*, to be
called "The *Formartine and Buchan* Railway."

[23d *July* 1858.]

WHEREAS the making of a Railway from the *Great North of
Scotland* Railway in the Parish of *Dyce* to the Parish of
Old Deer, and thence to the Towns of *Peterhead* and
Fraserburgh, with a Branch Railway to *Ellon*, all in the County of
Aberdeen, or partly in the County of *Aberdeen* and partly in the
County of *Banff*, would be attended with great local and public Advan-
tage: And whereas a Plan and Section of the intended Railways
showing the Lines and Levels thereof, with a Book of Reference to the
Plan containing the Names of the Owners or reputed Owners, Lessees
or reputed Lessees, and of the Occupiers of the Lands through which the
said Railways will pass, have been deposited with the Principal Sheriff
Clerk for the County of *Aberdeen*, and with the Principal Sheriff Clerk
for the County of *Banff*: And whereas the Persons herein-after named,
with others, are willing, at their own Expense, to construct the said

Opening to Peterhead and Fraserburgh

The Formartine & Buchan Railway Act of 23rd July 1858 incorporated the Company with a capital of £300,000 and borrowing powers of £100,000. The GNSR was given power to contribute up to £50,000. Several of the initial directors were also directors of the GNSR. Particular conditions were included in the Act to ensure that the railway works did not encroach on the harbour at Peterhead. Moreover, no part of the railway could be opened until the GNSR had doubled the line between Dyce and Kittybrewster and the Ellon branch had to open simultaneously with the line as far as Mintlaw. The Great North was authorised to work the F&B.

Raising the necessary capital was a problem from the start and took up a large part of the chairman's report to the first Ordinary Meeting on 2nd October 1858 in Aberdeen. The Great North had promised to construct the line provided £2,000 per mile was raised from landowners and others in the district through which it passed, or about £100,000 in all. Already £25,000 had been spent in the parliamentary contest to secure the Act.

It was realised at this stage that the branch to Ellon would add to both the capital and the working costs, so it was proposed to deviate the line to go by the outskirts of the town. To do that, another Bill was promoted in the ensuing session and this passed without difficulty and received Royal Assent on 19th April 1859.

The F&B directors did the rounds of the district in the Spring of 1859 to drum up support but there were problems. For instance, 7½ miles of the line were on the estates of the Earl of Aberdeen; while he was quite happy to let the railway pass through his lands, he refused to make any contribution despite having previously promised to do so. His tenants, 'a wealthy and well-to-do set of people' in the words of the F&B chairman, followed their landlord's lead. The *Peterhead Sentinel* several times discussed the question 'Are we to have a railway?'

By the beginning of July, sufficient support had been obtained to commence construction of the line as far as Mintlaw; the lines on to Peterhead and Fraserburgh would have to wait until more local support emerged. The contract for construction was let in July to Messrs Milne & Leslie for the portion from Dyce to Ellon and in September for the section on to Mintlaw, with completion expected in March 1861.

Most of the construction was fairly easy even if some deep cuttings were required, but there were two major bridges, a three arch one over the Don at Parkhill and one across the Ythan at Ellon. The laying of the keystone of the last of the three arches in the latter was a cause for ceremony and was performed on 2nd October 1860 by Charles N Gordon of Esslemont, followed by a few speeches. However, the structure did not last; a slip in the foundations of the abutment on the south bank brought it all down. The bridge was rebuilt with four arches, and by then the rest of the railway was ready for opening.

The mandatory Board of Trade inspection was carried out by Col Yolland on 10th and 11th July 1861. He issued a lengthy report.

He noted that the line was single throughout, no land having been purchased for a double line except at stations and passing places, and the over and under bridges and viaducts had only been constructed for single line except where

The viaduct at Ellon, which caused so much trouble during the construction of the line, still stands and is now part of the Formartine & Buchan Way.   (Keith Fenwick)

they were at stations, etc. The width of the railway at formation level was 15 feet.

The permanent way was of a substantial description and consisted of double headed rail weighing 72 lbs per yard in lengths of 21 ft fixed in cast iron chairs respectively weighing 22 lbs for the joint and 21 lbs for the intermediate chairs, the joints also being fished with two plates and four bolts and nuts together weighing 24 lbs per pair, a cast iron key being made use of at the joint chairs. The chairs were fastened to transverse sleepers of larch 9 ft long by 10 ins by 5 ins placed 3 ft apart from centre to centre by means of iron spikes, the rails being secured into the intermediate chairs by means of oak keys. The ballast was of gravel and broken stone and was stated to be 21 ins deep.

Yolland noted 23 under and 28 over bridges besides 22 viaducts over rivers, streams, brooks, etc.

Of the under bridges six were constructed entirely of stone and brick, and 27 had masonry abutments and cast iron girders;

the largest span was 35 ft on the square. Of the other bridges one half were built entirely of stone and brick and the other half had masonry abutments and cast iron girders; the largest span was 15 ft on the square and 16 2/3 ft. on the skew.

Of the viaducts, six were constructed entirely of stone and brick and the reminder had stone abutments and cast iron girders. The most important works were the viaducts over the Rivers Don and Ythan. The former consisted of three arches of 50 ft span and the viaduct over the River Ythan of three arches of 60 ft span and one of 35 ft span. The whole of the bridges and viaduct were well constructed and sufficiently strong. There were no unauthorised level crossings on the line and several of these which were sanctioned by Parliament had been done away with. Turntables had been erected at Ellon and Mintlaw stations. No turntable had been erected at Dyce Junction, but he was informed that all trains for the Formartine & Buchan Railway were to run from Aberdeen station and also that an engine turntable was to be erected at this junction in the event of that at Aberdeen getting out of order.

Stations had been constructed at Parkhill, Newmachar, Udny, Newburgh Turnpike Road, Esslemont, Ellon, Arnage, Auchnagatt, New Deer (i.e. Maud) and Old Deer and Mintlaw.

He noted that gradient boards had still to be put up. The cast iron girders for the six under bridges of small openings though strong enough for the engines proposed to be used at present were not strong enough for certain other engines now in the Company's possession which might be required to be used in an emergency. Under the circumstances these girders were to be

---

GREAT NORTH OF SCOTLAND RAILWAY.

FORMARTINE AND BUCHAN RAILWAY.

OPENING OF THE SECTION FOR PASSENGER AND GOODS TRAFFIC

BETWEEN

ABERDEEN AND OLD DEER AND MINTLAW STATION.

ON THURSDAY, the 18th July, 1861, until further notice, TRAINS will be worked as under, viz :—

DOWN TRAINS. Will not depart from	1 Mixed 1 & 3	2 Goods Pass & Parl. 1 & 3	3 Mixed 1 & 3	4 Goods & Pass 1 & 3	UP TRAINS. Will not depart from	1 Mixed 1 & 3	2 Goods Pass & Parl. 1 & 3	3 Mixed 1 & 3	4 Mixed 1 & 3
MAIN LINE.	A.M.	P.M.	P.M.	P.M.	FORMARTINE & BUCHAN.				
Aberdeen, *before*	8·55	12·40	3·20	6·0		A.M.	A.M.	P.M.	P.M.
Kittybrewster	9·3	12·48	3·28	6·8	Old Deer & Mintlaw *depart*	7·20	11·20	3·10	5·50
Woodside	9·6	—	—	6·11	Brucklay	7·31	11·31	3·21	6·1
Buxburn	9·12	12·56	—	6·15	Auchnagatt	7·46	11·47	3·36	6·16
Dyce Junction, *arrive*	9·18	1·3	3·43	6·22	Arnage	7·59	12·2	3·49	6·29
FORMARTINE & BUCHAN.					Ellon	8·12	12·17	4·2	6·42
					Esslemont	8·18	12·23	4·8	6·48
Dyce Junction, *depart*	9·20	1·5	3·47	6·24	Newburgh Road	8·24	12·29	4·14	6·54
Parkhill	9·24	1·9	3·51	6·29	Udny	8·30	12·36	4·18	6·58
Newmachar	9·40	1·25	4·7	6·47	Newmachar	8·41	12·46	4·31	7·10
Udny	9·50	1·35	4·18	6·58	Parkhill	8·53	12·58	4·43	7·22
Newburgh Road	9·55	1·40	4·23	7·4	Dyce Junction, *arrive*	8·58	1·5	4·48	7·27
Esslemont	10·0	1·46	4·28	7·10	MAIN LINE.				
Ellon	10·7	1·53	4·34	7·20	Dyce Junction, *depart*	9·0	1·7	4·50	7·30
Arnage	10·17	2·4	4·45	7·30	Buxburn	9·6	1·13	—	7·36
Auchnagatt	10·29	2·16	4·56	7·44	Woodside	9·11	1·18	5·1	7·41
Brucklay	10·44	2·32	5·12	8·0	Kittybrewster	9·16	1·37	5·6	7·46
Old Deer & Mintlaw, *arrive*	10·55	2·45	5·25	8·15	Aberdeen, *arrive*	9·25	1·45	5·15	7·55

NO SUNDAY TRAINS.

COACHES IN CONNECTION WITH THE TRAINS.

TO ABERDEEN, &c.

Leave PETERHEAD	for OLD DEER and MINTLAW	at	6·0 A.M.	10·0 A.M.	4·20 P.M.
„ FRASERBURGH	for do. do.	at	5·30 „	—	—
„ do.	for BRUCKLAY	at	—	—	3·45 „
„ CRUDEN	for ELLON	at	6·45 „	—	—
„ NEWBURGH	for NEWBURGH ROAD STATION	at	7·25 „	—	5·55 „
	ABERDEEN arrive by Rail	at	9·25 A.M.	1·45 P.M.	7·55 P.M.

FROM ABERDEEN, &c.

	ABERDEEN depart by Rail	at	8·55 A.M.	3·20 P.M.	6·0 P.M.
Leave NEWBURGH ROAD STATION	for NEWBURGH	at	10·0 „	—	7·10 „
„ ELLON	for CRUDEN	at	—	4·40 „	—
„ BRUCKLAY	for FRASERBURGH	at	10·55 „	—	—
„ OLD DEER and MINTLAW	for do.	at	—	5·30 „	—
„ do. do.	for PETERHEAD	at	11·0 A.M.	5·50 P.M.	8·20 P.M.

Coach and Railway Tickets to be had of Mr W. L. TAYLOR, Bookseller, Railway Coach Office, Peterhead.

For Passenger Fares, Conditions under which Tickets are issued, Regulations for Collection and Delivery of Goods, &c., see Great North of Scotland Railway Company's Time Tables.

The Agents at the various Stations, and Messrs PICKFORD & Co., Aberdeen and Peterhead, will give information as to Rates for the Conveyance of Goods, Live Stock, &c.

By order,

ROBERT MILNE, General Manager.

Aberdeen, 12th July, 1861.

taken out and replaced by stronger ones before the line was opened for traffic.

The over bridges which were constructed with cast iron girders were not strong enough to carry a traction engine or a truck although he did not recommend any action.

He expressed some concern over the Ythan viaduct as there was evidence of some subsidence since the centering had been taken down three weeks before; he wanted it to be carefully watched but approved the line for opening.

Newmachar and Udny were constructed on steep and long inclines of 1 in 70 and 1 in 80. An Up siding was to be constructed within three months at the former station and blind sidings at both. New Deer was constructed on an incline of 1 in 100 but it would be difficult to provide protection so he insisted that two trains should not be on the line between Old Deer, Mintlaw and Auchnagatt stations. Udny loop was not yet finished.

The line was in very good order and he therefore passed the line for opening.

But he added that the junction signals at Dyce differed from these usually employed at junctions. He was not prepared to say that they were to prove insufficient, but he would strongly urge for the consideration of the directors that the use system of establishing a signal box at the junction should be adopted, the signalman to have the complete control of the signals and the telegraphing in each direction instead of dividing the responsibility between the station agent and one or two signalmen.

With commendable speed, services started on Thursday 18th July with four trains each way and coaches in connection to Peterhead, Fraserburgh and various other places. There was little ceremony; the *Peterhead Sentinel* remarked that the first train was long and well filled but even so arrived in Aberdeen on time. Everything was neat and tidy and the guards and porters at all the stations civil and obliging. Even the third class carriages, four wheelers with wooden seats, were favourably commented on for their comfort

Peterhead from the main road just north of the station showing the line to the harbour in the foreground, with protection iron gates made by Harper & Co. The station building in the background is in its original condition, a plain building without overall roof.   (GNSRA collection)

and ventilation. The Great North operated the line and provided all the rolling stock.

The original service of four trains each way was reduced after a few months to three plus one as far as Ellon.

Failure to complete the line to Peterhead continued to worry the leader writer of the *Peterhead Sentinel* in articles during 1860. Encouraged by progress on the line to Mintlaw, £15,000 out of the £20,000 needed had been raised by the time of the annual meeting in November 1860, and the directors believed that they would shortly be able to carry the line on to Peterhead. Local support gradually increased, so construction eventually commenced on 22nd July 1861 with completion expected by June the following year. At Peterhead, the station was to be sited on the north side of the town, next to the Fraserburgh turnpike.

Work proceeded without major problems and the line was ready for the Board of Trade inspection by Col Rich on 30th June 1862. He noted that there was a passing place at Longside and numerous sidings at Peterhead. Single platform stations were provided at Newseat and Inverugie. Switches were of ordinary pattern. There was one public level crossing which was equipped with gates to close across the line and a good lodge for the gatekeeper. The line was provided with Tyer's Electric Telegraph instruments. A turntable was installed at Peterhead and indicators were attached to the facing points.

Opening followed on Thursday July 3rd by the simple process of extending the trains from Mintlaw. The first train left Peterhead at 7.35am in the presence of about 1,000 spectators. The journey from Peterhead to Aberdeen now took about 2 hours 40 minutes.

The *Peterhead Sentinel* published a guide book for travellers on the new line, in the expectation of tourist traffic developing. It lauded the town: 'we know of no town of its size along the eastern coast of Scotland where a tourist may more enjoy himself

Great North of Scotland Railway.

FORMARTINE & BUCHAN SECTION.

OPENING of the PETERHEAD EXTENSION

ON THURSDAY, the 3d JULY, 1862, the Trains were extended from OLD DEER and MINTLAW STATION to PETERHEAD, working through with Aberdeen, as under —

DOWN TRAINS.

Will not Depart from	Goods and Passengers 1 & 3 Class.	Mixed and Parl 1 & 3	Mixed 1 & 3 Class.
	A.M.	P.M.	P.M.
Aberdeen (Waterloo) before	8·50	1 40	6·30
Ellon	10·2	3 0	7·37
Old Deer and Mintlaw	10·50	4·51	8 30
Longside	11 0	4·1	8·42
Newseat	11 6	4·7	8·48
Inverugie	11·12	4·13	8 55
Arrive at			
Peterhead	11·20	4·20	9 5

UP TRAINS.

Will not depart from	Mixed 1 & 3 Class.	Mixed and Parl 1 & 3 Class	Goods and Pass 1 & 3 Class.
	A.M.	A.M.	P M
Peterhead before	7·35	11 40	5·20
Inverugie	7·41	11·46	5·26
Newseat	7·47	11·52	5·32
Longside	7·66	12·0	6·40
Old Deer and Mintlaw	8·9	12·10	6·52
Ellon	9·4	12·50	6·40
Arrive at			
Aberdeen	10·15	2·10	8·0

For Passenger Fares, Conditions under which Tickets are issued, Time at Stations on the Main Line and Branches, connection at Dyce Junction, and other particulars, see Company's Time Tables for the month.

The Agents at the Stations will supply rates and charges for the conveyance of Goods and Live Stock, or they may be obtained of Messrs Pickford & Co., the Company's Agents at Peterhead, Aberdeen, London, &c., and at the Traffic Manager's Office, Waterloo Station, Aberdeen.

Goods and Live Stock are booked at Through Rates by Railway and Steamers between Peterhead and London *via* Aberdeen.

By order,
ROBERT MILNE, Gen. Manager.

Aberdeen, 27th June, 1862.

Timetable from 3rd July 1862, published in *Peterhead Sentinel*, 14 July 1862.

for a couple of days in the summer than in Peterhead ... (and) enjoy the sea breeze to the utmost advantage.'

The *Sentinel* also remarked on the neat appearance of the line, giving one of the reasons the wire fencing by Harper & Co. of Aberdeen consisting of 6 strands of galvanised wire rope tensioned by cast iron posts placed on average 13 yards apart. Charred larch posts about 7 feet apart supported the wires between them. Harper also provided the iron gates on the line.

Powers for land purchase by the F&B expired in July 1861 with no progress made

GREAT NORTH OF SCOTLAND RAILWAY.

FORMARTINE AND BUCHAN SECTION.

OPENING OF

FRASERBURGH EXTENSION

FOR TRAFFIC.

REDUCTION OF PASSENGER FARES.

ON MONDAY, 24th April, 1865, and until further notice, Trains will arrive and depart as under:—

Down Trains—To Fraserburgh, Peterhead &c.   **Up Trains—From Peterhead, Fraserburgh, &c.**

STATIONS.	Pass. 1 & 3	Pass. 1 & 3	Pass. 1 & 3	Pass. 1 & 3	Pass. Part. 1 & 3	Pass. 1 & 3 Fridays & Sat. only.	Pass. 1 & 3 Fridays & Sat. only.	Pass. 1 & 3
	A.M.	A.M.	A.M.	P.M.	P.M.	P.M.	P.M.	P.M.
Aberdeen, depart	..	6 30	8 40	..	1 50	3 0	..	4 0
Kittybrewster	..	6 39	8 49	..	1 55	3 7	..	4 8
Woodside	..	6 33	8 53	..	2 2	3 11	..	6 12
Buxburn	..	6 39	8 59	..	2 9	3 16	..	6 17
Dyce Jun., arrive	..	6 46	9 13	..	2 16	3 22	..	6 23
Dyce Jun., depart	..	6 50	9 16	..	2 20	3 24	..	6 25
Parkhill	..	6 54	9 20	..	2 24	3 29	..	6 29
Newmachar	..	7 7	9 32	..	2 38	3 41	..	6 44
Udny	..	7 16	9 41	..	2 47	3 50	..	6 55
Logierieve	..	7 20	9 45	..	2 51	3 54	..	6 59
Esslemont	..	7 25	9 50	..	2 5	3 59	..	7 4
Ellon	..	7 33	9 53	..	3 3	4 5	..	7 12
Arnage	..	7 44	10 5	..	3 17	..	..	7 25
Auchnagatt	..	7 57	10 18	..	3 30	..	..	7 37
New Maud Ju. ar. formerly Brucklay	..	8 12	10 30	..	3 43	..	..	7 50
New Maud Ju. de.	7 16	8 15	10 33	..	3 50	..	6 10	7 53
O. Deer & Mintw.	7 27	8 26	10 44	..	4 5	..	6 21	8 5
Longside	7 37	8 36	10 54	..	4 15	..	6 30	8 15
Newseat	7 57	8 46	10 59	..	4 20	..	6 34	8 18
Inverugie	7 45	8 43	11 5	..	4 26	..	6 40	8 23
Peterhead, arrive	7 55	8 55	11 15	..	4 36	..	6 50	8 36
New Maud Ju. de.	7 5	..	10 33	11 15	3 50	..	..	7 53
Brucklay	7 10	..	10 38	11 19	3 54	..	..	7 57
Strichen	7 26	..	10 44	11 31	4 0	..	..	8 10
Mormond	7 36	..	10 54	11 39	4 14	..	..	8 18
Lonmay ar.	7 44	..	11 2	11 47	4 21	..	..	8 25
Rathen	7 54	..	11 10	11 55	4 28	..	..	8 32
Fraserburgh, ar.	8 10	..	11 25	12 10	4 40	..	..	8 45

STATIONS.	Pass. 1 & 3	Pass. Part. 1 & 3	Pass. 1 & 3	Pass. 1 & 3	Pass. 1 and 3 Fridays & Sat. only	Pass. 1 and 3 Fridays & Sat. only
	A.M.	A.M.	P.M.	P.M.	P.M.	P.M.	P.M.
Peterhead, depart	6 15	9 23	12 20	..	..	5 20	7 5
Inverugie	6 23	9 30	12 34	..	..	5 25	7 9
Newseat	6 30	9 34	12 28	..	..	5 29	7 13
Longside	6 33	9 43	12 33	3 15	..	5 34	7 20
Old Deer & Mintlaw	6 43	9 51	12 45	3 24	..	5 44	7 30
New Maud Ju., ar. formerly Brucklay	6 54	10 3	12 56	3 35	..	5 57	7 45
Fraserburgh, depart	6 6	9 15	12 0	..	..	5 6	..
Rathen	6 9	9 23	12 8	..	..	5 13	..
Lonmay	6 15	9 30	12 15	..	..	5 20	..
Mormond	6 24	9 38	12 22	..	..	5 27	..
Strichen	6 32	9 45	12 29	..	..	5 34	..
Brucklay	6 44	9 55	12 3	..	..	5 46	..
New Maud Ju., ar.	6 53	10 3	12 50	..	..	5 55	..
New Maud Ju., dep.	7 0	10 6	1 2	3 58	..	6 0	..
Auchnagatt	7 12	10 16	1 9	..	..	6 12	..
Arnage	7 24	10 27	1 20	..	..	6 24	..
Ellon	7 35	10 34	1 32	..	4 25	6 33	..
Esslemont	7 40	10 43	1 37	..	4 30	6 4	..
Logierieve	7 45	10 49	1 42	..	..	6 45	..
Udny	7 50	10 53	1 48	..	4 40	6 53	..
Newmachar	8 1	11 4	2 0	..	4 49	7 9	..
Parkhill	8 15	11 15	2 14	..	6 0	7 17	..
Dyce Junction, arrive	8 20	11 19	2 20	..	5 4	7 21	..
Dyce Junction, dep.	8 24	11 22	2 22	..	5 5	7 24	..
Buxburn	8 30	11 28	2 29	..	5 11	7 29	..
Woodside	8 36	11 29	2 32	..	..	7 34	..
Kittybrewster	8 48	11 34	2 47	..	5 21	7 41	..
Aberdeen, arrive	8 55	11 40	2 56	..	5 30	7 50	..

Return Tickets at One and a Half Ordinary Fares daily, available to return on day of issue.
Return Tickets on SATURDAYS, at One Ordinary Fare, available to return on day of issue or on MONDAY following.

Cheap Fares for Fisherwomen.

Third Class Tickets at One Ordinary Fare issued to Fisherwomen at Fraserburgh, Rathen, Lonmay, and Peterhead, to Aberdeen or any intermediate Station, available to return on day of issue or day following. One Creel load of Fish allowed to each free of charge, and any additional Package charged Goods' Rates.

Passengers Booked Through from Peterhead and Fraserburgh to Edinburgh, Glasgow, London, &c.

Cheap Fares to Edinburgh.

On THURSDAYS Passengers are Booked Third Class from Fraserburgh by 12·0 P.M. Train, and from Peterhead by 12·20 P.M. Train, to Edinburgh at 13s. 6d.

Goods Traffic.

Information as to Rates, Delivery of Goods, &c., &c., will be obtained on application to the Traffic Manager, Waterloo Station, Aberdeen, the Agents at the respective Stations, or Messrs Mutter, Howe & Company, Agents for the Company, at Fraserburgh, Peterhead, Aberdeen, &c.

For further particulars, Condition on which Tickets are issued, &c., &c., see the Company's Time Tables.

By Order,

ROBERT MILNE, Gen. Manager.

COMPANY'S OFFICE,
Waterloo Station, Aberdeen, 20th April, 1865.

on the line to Fraserburgh. A public meeting there in February 1862 confirmed that there was local support. Whether the line should go to the east or west of Mormond Hill was discussed, but several landowners made the eastern route a condition of their support. This reflected one of the problems of serving Buchan, the dispersed nature of its towns and villages. By April, £22,000 had been raised on the basis that the eastern route would be followed. Further support was generated during the year, so that by November 1862, the F&B was able to deposit a Bill to construct the line from Maud to Fraserburgh via Strichen and the east of Mormond Hill. This allowed an additional £100,000 capital to be raised as preference shares.

The first sod was cut in August 1863 with construction proceeding smoothly if not very quickly. The Board of Trade inspection report was dated 24th April 1865. The inspector, Captain Tyler, stated that the single headed rails weighed 65 lbs to the yard and were 24 ft long. The chairs and sleepers were similar to that used previously on the F&B. Most bridges were constructed with cast iron beams and masonry abutments with a maximum span of 37 ft 6 ins. They were tested with two engines funnel to funnel. There were no crossing places on the line, the intention being to work it by one engine in steam. He recommended that a raised platform be constructed at Maud Junction with locking apparatus on the system of either Saxby & Farmer or Messrs Stephens at the point of the junction and proper means of communication be provided between the junction and the station. The Company undertook to do so within three months; in the meantime traffic could be worked at very low speed over the facing point.

The line opened on 24th April 1865 with, on this occasion suitable celebrations. A special train ran from Aberdeen on Saturday 22nd conveying directors and others to dinner in the Commissioners' Hall at Fraserburgh. The train arrived 10 minutes early at Fraserburgh, too early for the planned formal reception which was cancelled. Nor were the Volunteers, who were to line the streets, ready in time! The whole town turned out in holiday mood although the following Monday had been declared a holiday to mark the actual opening. The usual lengthy speeches were made at the dinner.

Both Peterhead and Fraserburgh had important harbours, not only for the fishing trade by which they later became famous, but also for bringing in goods for their respective localities and taking out produce. It was felt important to connect the railway to the harbours as an extension to the shipping services. In practice, the railways took away much of the coastal shipping traffic. At Fraserburgh, enlargement of the harbour ensured the two were linked. At Peterhead, an extension of the line was needed, estimated to cost £9,000. There was much discussion as to whether this would go round the north or south side of the town and just where the junction with the main line would be made. In the end a route round the north side of the town was agreed, connecting directly into the goods yard. The F&B agreed to build it if £3,000 was raised locally and the Harbour Trustees were responsible for laying rails on the quays. It was not until late in 1864 that this was finally resolved and construction could begin. The extension was opened on 9th August 1865; it never carried any passenger traffic.

The F&B had been promoted as a separate company to ensure that some of its capital could be raised locally. Other branch lines throughout the north east were promoted in the same way, so by 1865, the GNSR found itself operating the lines of nine other companies and it had considerable financial stakes in most of them. All this was an administrative burden and a source of financial confusion, so the company sought parliamentary powers in 1865 to absorb the branch line companies, including the F&B. The Act was authorised

Thus photograph of Fraserburgh was taken when the line opened and formed the basis of an engraving which was published in the *Banffshire Journal.* It is difficult to know where the photographer was standing to gain such height. The harbour is to the right. The locomotive shed in the centre still survives; adapted for commercial use some years after the line closed, it is now only just recognisable behind secure fencing. The original station is to its right.   (GNSRA collection)

in July 1866, and the F&B ceased to exist as an independent company at that time. Its name did live on as many documents continued to refer to the F&B or, later, to the Buchan section of the GNSR.

Accounts for the F&B were published annually. The final accounts, to 31 July 1866, show that about £350,000 had been spent on building the line to Peterhead and a further £124,000 on the Fraserburgh extension. This capital expenditure was funded by £140,000 raised in ordinary shares, £100,000 in preference shares issued to the GNSR and £100,000 in debenture loans. The balance was covered by various temporary loans, including £77,000 from the company's bankers.

The Revenue account for the final year showed that total income was £26,283, of which just under half came from goods and live stock. Operating expenses totalled £15,055, the rest of the revenue being taken up by interest payments. Dividends had been paid in some years, 1¼% 1862, 1½% in 1863 and 1865, but nothing in 1864 or 1866 due to high bank interest rates.

All in all, the financial position of the F&B was poor. It had never been properly funded from ordinary shares and had to rely on borrowing both from the GNSR and bankers. At least a small dividend had been paid, unlike some of the other branch line companies worked by the GNSR. The amalgamations of 1866 swept away this financial muddle and allowed the Great North to consolidate its accounts. However, it did so in the middle of a financial crisis which drove bank rates up to a very high level. The Great North was lucky to escape bankruptcy in 1866, but that is another story.

LATER PROPOSALS AND DEVELOPMENTS

There was to be no more railway building in Buchan for 40 years, but like various parts of the country, the area had its share of proposals which came to nothing. The early idea of a railway following the coast to Newburgh and then up the Ythan valley to Ellon was rejected on the grounds that the area would be better served if the railway went up the middle, although it did mean that the coastal area south of Peterhead, including towns such as Newburgh, were well away. A steam tramway was proposed in the mid-1870s to run from Aberdeen via Newburgh, Collieston, Cruden, Burnhaven and Boddam to Peterhead. By offering a shorter route to Peterhead, transport to Aberdeen would be cheaper. It would be run along the centre of the roads. Similar tramways were common in Europe but the idea did not take on in Britain and this scheme failed to gain much support. Newburgh was eventually served by motor bus services operated by the GNSR.

When the Buchan line was built, the then Lord Aberdeen would have nothing to do with it. However, his son realised that this had been a mistake and that the estates would benefit from rail connection. In October 1879 he wrote to the Great North Board with a proposal to build a railway at his own expense from Udny to Methlick, some 10 miles away, the completed line to be taken over and worked by the Great North. The necessary Bill was laid before Parliament later the same year, However, due to rising costs and local controversy, his Lordship abandoned the Bill early in 1880. This is described in detail in David Fasken's *The Earl of Aberdeen's Railway* (published by the Association).

Means of serving fishing villages along the coast led to a proposal to build a line from Fraserburgh westward to Rosehearty and New Aberdour and the GNSR obtained an Act in 1884 for this line, a distance of about 9 miles, but the powers were never exercised and so lapsed.

The Light Railways Act of 1896 generated a flurry of proposals in Buchan, as in other parts of the country. In 1900 there was a proposal for a light railway to run from Udny or Logierieve to Tarves or Methlick which, interestingly, would be powered by electricity generated in a hydro-electric plant on the river Ythan. Later, in 1908, a syndicate was formed to make a second attempt to build a line to New Aberdour. The Treasury promised a grant and arrangements were made with the GNSR to work it, but once again nothing came of the idea.

In the early 1890s there was considerable discussion about a railway following a west to east route to fill in the gap west of the line to Fraserburgh; there was even a suggestion for one to more or less follow the coast to serve the various fishing villages and which would at the same time provide a direct coast route from Fraserburgh to Inverness. However, geographical difficulties quickly put an end to such an idea.

Particular interest was shown in the possibility of a railway some 12 miles long connecting Maud with Turriff on the Macduff line. In 1890 the Great North was pressurised to support this proposal since for some obscure reason there was speculation that the North British Railway might be interested. The project was raised again in 1894, this time as a narrow gauge line. Again nothing happened. Then in 1914 it was just possible that it might have succeeded as it was supported by the Scottish Light Railways & Development Syndicate. The intervening country was prosperous farming

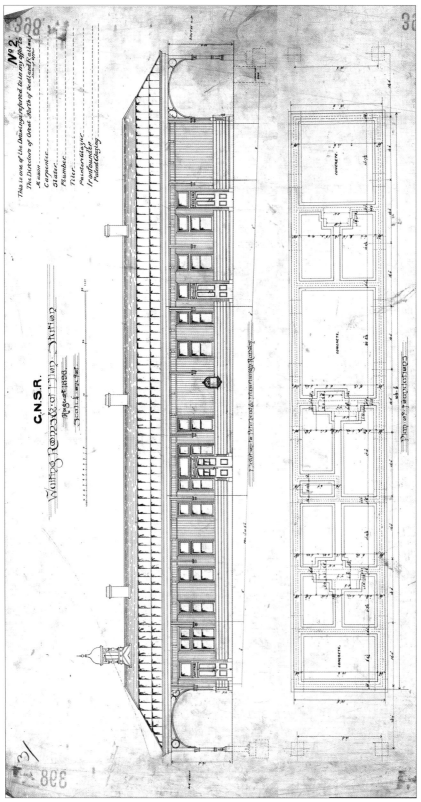

The construction of the Cruden line led to expansion at Ellon. The main building, in stone, remained on the Down platform while the Up platform was rebuilt with a bay for the branch trains and this extensive wooden building housing a general waiting room, First and Third class ladies' waiting room, First Class gentlemen's waiting room, porters and guards rooms. Urinals at the north end had an elaborate cupola for ventilation. (GNSRA collection)

land and it received the blessing of the Board of Agriculture for Scotland, the Light Railways Commission and the Treasury, but the outbreak of war later that year brought further progress to a stop.

The need for a railway to serve the district lying to the east of Ellon continued to be discussed. The directors were not convinced that such a railway was justified as they regarded the traffic prospects as being poor. However by the early 1890s there were hopes of development at Cruden Bay and nearby Port Errol. A route was surveyed and authorised by Act of Parliament in 1893 for a railway 15¼ miles long from Ellon to Boddam, a fishing village 3 miles south of Peterhead. There were no great constructional difficulties and the line was opened on 2nd August 1897.

Pressure to continue the line to Peterhead continued over the years, but the expenditure could not be justified as the shorter distance would lead to reduced revenue from Peterhead traffic.

In August 1890 the Board had obtained parliamentary powers to operate hotels and in January 1895 decided to investigate the possibility of building a luxury establishment

near Port Errol. Eventually a site was chosen at Cruden Bay, an ideal location having a fine bay with a magnificent sandy beach. Building started in late 1896 and the 75 bedroom hotel opened on 1st March 1899. Nearby an 18 hole golf course, designed by "Old Tom" Morris of St. Andrews was laid out with an adjoining 9 hole course intended at that time for lady players. Upgraded over the years Cruden Bay is still counted among Scotland's great links courses.

By the late 1890s, there was a considerable expansion of the fishing industry based on Fraserburgh, so much so that local business interests proposed a railway from there to St. Combs, a fishing village about 5 miles to the south-east, passing through the neighbouring village of Inverallochy. A Light Railway Order was obtained by the GNSR in September 1899 but for some reason construction was delayed so that the line did not open until 1st July 1903.

The final proposals came from the Report of the Rural Transport (Scotland) Committee which reported in 1919 and again proposed a line from Turriff to Maud together with one from Fraserburgh to New Aberdour, but nothing came of that report.

An early postcard showing the Cruden Bay Hotel.   (Ross Kerby collection)

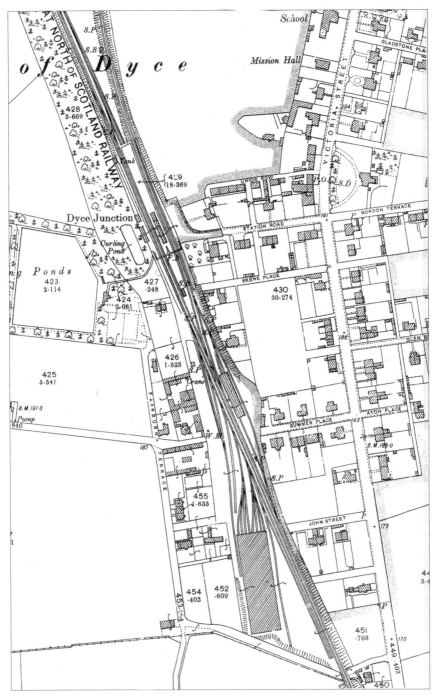

Dyce on the 1902 OS map. By that time, a substantial carriage shed had been built to the south of the station.

Along the Line to Peterhead

The junction between the Buchan line and the Great North main line was about ¼ mile on the Aberdeen side of the existing station at Dyce which led to a new one being built to serve the village with four platforms, two on each line. Although the line from Aberdeen to Dyce was doubled just after the opening of the F&B as one of the conditions of the Act authorising it, the F&B itself was single with passing places at most stations.

From Dyce, the line dropped down to cross the River Don on a handsome three arch stone bridge, just beyond which was the first station at Parkhill (1¼ miles) built to serve the surrounding area but nowhere in particular. Little is known about the station itself, except that it had a single platform on the Up side and small goods yard on the Down side, as no photographs of it when in use have come to light.

The only section of double track commenced just north of Parkhill station and extended for 1½ miles to Elrick, used seasonally between 1920 and 1925. In the 1950s, it was the site of a signal gantry with no less than six arms which was used for eyesight testing.

The line now began a steep climb through Newmachar (5¼ miles), which was fairly close to the village on the Oldmeldrum road and had a crossing loop and a neat stone station house on the Down platform. Several stations along the line had similar buildings which provided basic accommodation for the staff and passengers. A central entrance gave access to a 'waiting shed' which was open on the platform side and was flanked by a booking office on one side and a waiting room on the

The viaduct over the Don at Parkhill, viewed from the south bank of the river on the west side in June 2002.
(Keith Fenwick)

The local lads have obviously been told to keep out of the way as an Up train enters Newmachar in Great North days. Two signal boxes were provided here in 1890; the north box seen above also controlled the sidings beyond. The footbridge was a standard GNSR design in wood. These rotted in time, and were all replaced in the 1930s by ones built from old rails, typical LNER careful control of expenditure.

(Bob Drummond collection)

other. Later the waiting area was enclosed behind a wood and glass screen on the platform side to provide more comfort for waiting passengers. The waiting room gave access to a WC and was reserved for women. Adjacent but with outside access were a men's urinal and WC. On the Up platform, a small shelter provided protection for passengers; this was also originally open fronted, but the Board of Trade persuaded the company to enclose the front in the 1880s. When the line opened, station agents were expected to find their own accommodation locally, but this was not always easy. In the 1870s, the Company provided proper houses for agents at most stations; many of these survive today. At some places houses were available for purchase, such as the one at Newmachar which was bought from the local GP.

Beyond Newmachar, the line climbed on to reach the summit of almost 450 feet where it passed through the Hill of Strypes

in a cutting nearly a mile long and up to 50 feet deep - the cause of many problems during heavy snow. Udny (8¼ miles) was a couple of miles from the village of that name although actually in the parish of Foveran, but a small settlement grew up around the station, still known as Udny Station today. The station house, on the Up side, was similar to that at Newmachar. A loop was provided here, but initially there was only one platform. The Down platform was added later. Beside the station was a hotel which the Company owned at one time but was later sold. Udny would have became a junction in later years if the proposed railway to Methlick had materialised.

The line continued northwards through two isolated stations. Logierieve (10 miles), had a single platformed station with a small goods yard; originally called Newburgh Road it was re-named after about a year as that place was about 5 miles away. Esslemont (11½ miles), like Logierieve,

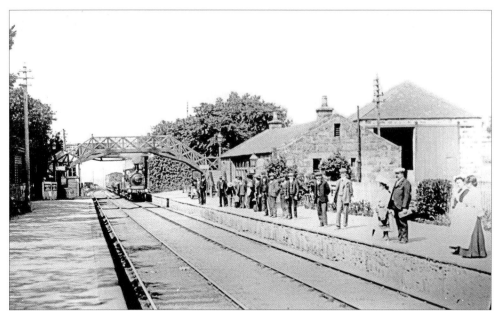

An Up train entering Udny in the early years of the 20th century. The trees are in full bloom, so it must have been summertime. The locomotive is No. 97, one of the T class built between 1895 and 1898. The train consists of several fitted open wagons for carrying fish followed by passenger coaches.

(GNSRA collection)

Logierieve, looking north in the 1950s. The signal box housed a ground frame which controlled access to the single siding in the foreground. Beyond the station building, which also provided compact living accommodation with a two storey extension at the rear, the Newburgh Road crossed the line.

(John A N Emslie/GNSRA

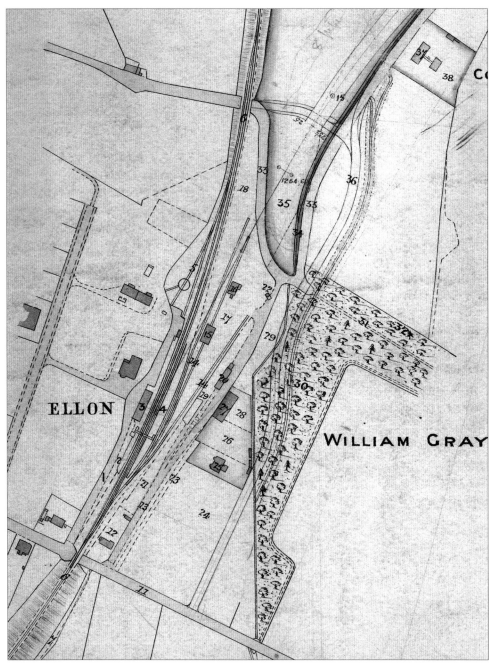

Ellon station from the working plans for the Cruden line shows the layout of the station before the Cruden line was built. The course of the Buchan line is shown in outline, as is ownership of adjacent land; for instance William Gray owned the land to the east of the station. The turntable shown was 22ft 7ins long, not much used, and disappeared between 1902 and 1916. New roads to the east of the station are outlined in red.   (GNSRA collection)

Esslemont was an isolated station in open countryside. At one time there was a loop on the right. By June 1969, when seen from the rear of an Up goods train, it had long been closed.
(Keith Fenwick)

had a stone building which provided living accommodation for the station agent in addition to public facilities. The roof space accommodated a bedroom, giving the buildings a larger appearance than those at Udny and Newmachar. A loop at Esslemont was provided in 1921 as part of the enhancements to cope with seasonal fish traffic. It saw seasonal use until 1925. The station closed to all traffic in 1952.

A couple of miles after Esslemont, the line crossed the River Ythan on a 4-arch viaduct illustrated on page 12, which as already noted was the cause of delays in opening the line, and reached Ellon.

Ellon, which had been the ancient capital of Buchan, was quite a small town when the railway arrived but is now greatly enlarged, acting as a dormitory town for Aberdeen. Unfortunately the line was closed before the recent expansion, otherwise some of the traffic problems at Bridge of Don might have been avoided. The original station here had a larger stone building on the Down platform with a long verandah supported on iron pillars which was never enclosed. In 1897 when it became the junction for the branch to Boddam, the Up platform

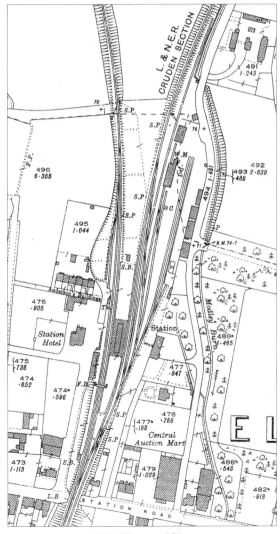

1926 OS map of Ellon

Ellon from the south end. The original station building is on the northbound platform to the left with the large water tank beyond it. Boddam branch trains used the platform on the right, to the right of which was the goods yard. Most of the site is now occupied by industrial development.   (LGRP)

Ellon looking north from the south end of the Down platform. The original building is on the left, with its long open verandah supported by iron pillars. Unlike most other stations on the line, this area was never enclosed behind a wooden screen, although a proposal to do so was made in LNER days. In complete contrast is the island platform building added for the Cruden line. Public access to the station remained via the original building so passengers from the town had to pass under the railway line and use the road on the west side of the line before tackling the footbridge.   (John Emslie/GNSRA)

Arnage in the 1950s looking north. The station was on a reverse curve with the main building on the Down platform. The building was originally open at the front but a wooden screen was later added to provide protection for waiting passengers. (John Emslie/GNSRA)

was converted into an island and provided with a wooden waiting room complete with substantial awnings on all sides. One clerk "had committed defalcations with his cash book to the extent of £7.10.8¾" and was dismissed but not before the money had been made good.

From Ellon, the railway continued through pleasant agricultural countryside with scattered steadings to reach Arnage (16¾ miles), then Auchnagatt (20¾ miles) where the Ellon to New Deer road crossed the line. Both these stations had stone buildings on the Down side and passing places which were added some time after the line opened. Auchnagatt is illustrated

An early postcard showing activity in the sidings at Auchnagatt. General goods are being unloaded from the open box wagon on the left, while on the right a well-limed roofless cattle wagon waits for its cargo. (GNSRA collection)

on the rear cover.

The line then ran down to Maud (25 miles), a place which owes much to the coming of the railway. Not only was it to be the junction of the branch to Fraserburgh with the attendant need for extra railway staff, but it became an important agricultural centre with no less than three auction marts. Long lines of cattle wagons would in time be crammed into the goods yard on the west side of the line. Maud started life as Brucklay, named after the castle a couple of miles away. It was renamed New Maud when the Fraserburgh line was opened in 1865 and finally Maud at the end of 1867. The layout of the station reflected the operational need to split and join trains which normally consisted of both Peterhead and Fraserburgh portions to and from Aberdeen.

The station house, another low stone building, was in the Y of the two lines with platforms on each line. It was designed for the Peterhead line as it had a verandah on that side; on the Fraserburgh side it always looked like the back of a building.

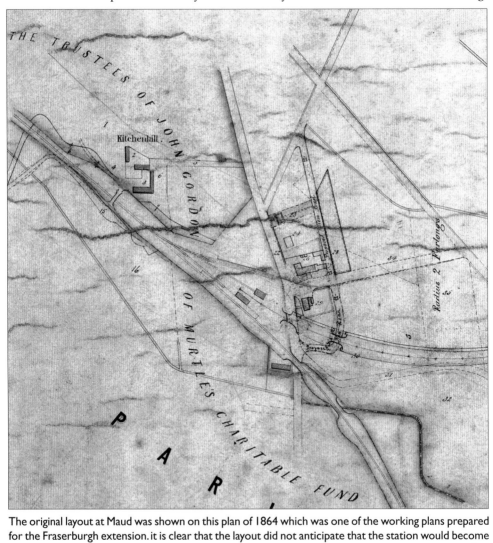

The original layout at Maud was shown on this plan of 1864 which was one of the working plans prepared for the Fraserburgh extension. it is clear that the layout did not anticipate that the station would become a junction. There was little room for the new track between the station building and the goods shed. The construction of the Fraserburgh line resulted in a diversion of what is now Deer Road and the building of a new road behind the houses, although that was not built as shown.   (GNSRA collection)

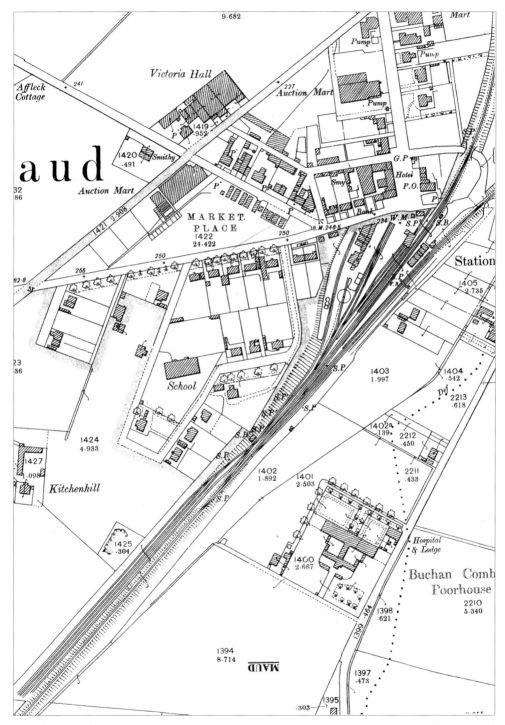

1902 OS Map of Maud. The layout has now reached the form which would remain basically unchanged until the 1960s, apart from the replacement of the two signal boxes by one at the south end of the Up Peterhead platform.

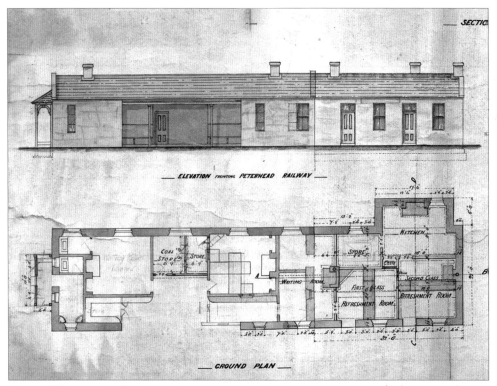

The original station building at Maud is shown on this plan of 1869 which includes, marked in red, the addition of a refreshment rooms. The elevation is from the Peterhead platform. All the early Buchan stations followed the same basic design of a single storey building with roughly dressed stone walls and a low-pitched roof. Narrow windows and an open-fronted waiting area were also features. (GNSRA)

A train entering the Peterhead platform in late Victorian days. It had stopped at the south end of the station to leave off the Fraserburgh coaches, which can be seen in the distance. The newsagents stall is to the right of the footbridge.   (Ross Kerby collection)

The original South box at Maud can be seen in this enlargement from part of a postcard taken from the hillside to the east of the town.

(K G Jones collection)

An extension was added in 1869 at the northern end to provide first and third class refreshment rooms and a kitchen; these were privately operated.

A loop on the Fraserburgh side had a narrow platform while on the Peterhead side a loop was proposed in 1880, when signalling alterations were estimated to cost £1,171. In 1882 it was agreed to provide a footbridge to the Up Peterhead platform together with a verandah on it which cost £67.12.0. A small goods yard and turntable were originally set up on the west side of the station, but several sidings were later added

Maud from the south end, showing the signal box built in 1935 to replace the separate north and south boxes on the right and to provide greater operational flexibility. From the right are the Peterhead Up platform, Down platform which was also used by trains terminating at Maud, Fraserburgh passenger platform used by trains in both directions and Fraserburgh goods loop, which was also used in both directions and was equipped by a platform with no passenger access so was presumably used for goods and parcels traffic. The sidings are mainly out of sight on the far left.   (John Emslie/GNSRA)

Maud was where the action took place, with the joining and splitting of trains and several sidings to shunt, especially on cattle market days. It was also very convenient for Sandy Murdoch who lived and worked locally and took these photos. A train runs in to the Up Fraserburgh platform while another, headed by a class D31 waits to set off to the north. On the right is the north signal box, abolished in 1935.

to handle livestock and agricultural traffic. In the 1970s, these were also used to handle pipelines for the north sea oil industry. Maud was the scene of a couple of suicides, both by drowning in the water tank. In 1912 William Rae, a postman, threw himself in it, while in 1913 William Strachan, a painter,

was found drowned in the same place.

From Maud, the line turned eastwards to follow the valley of the South Ugie Water towards Peterhead and passed the remains of Deer Abbey, a Cistercian monastery dating from early in the 13th century. For several years in the 1930s special trains ran to a small

The short platform at Abbey of Deer derelict by the time this photo was taken in the 1950s but clearly only limited use was expected of it.

(J L Stevenson)

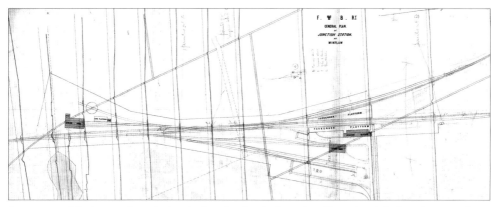

At one stage Mintlaw was intended as the junction for the branch to Fraserburgh before the more direct route from Maud was chosen. This plan was prepared by the F&B and survived because it shows the drainage at the station. A separate platform for the Fraserburgh line is shown with a run-round loop. A locomotive shed and turntable were planned at the west end. Another plan was prepared showing a two road engine shed opposite the branch platform. (GNSRA collection)

platform carrying pilgrims to the Abbey.

The next station was Mintlaw (29 miles) where the station was built half way between the settlements of Old Deer, just to the south of the line, and Mintlaw, on the Fraserburgh turnpike. The village which grew up around it was known as Mintlaw Station. The station was initially named Old Deer and Mintlaw and renamed in 1867. A larger station house, similar to that at Ellon, was built here. After closure of the station it remained derelict for many years and was then restored for office use but a subsequent fire left it again derelict. Eventually it was demolished. A substantial goods yard was built on the south side of the line.

A good turnout of village folk when the photographer came to Mintlaw. This is looking east, with the main building on the Up platform and a hipped-roof signal box in the distance. The wooden footbridge was a standard GNSR design but all had to be replaced in LNER days due to rotting timber.

(Sandy White/GNSRA collection)

An NB Type 2 shunts at Mintlaw in the early 1960s. Coal was still an important traffic at wayside stations, but was not enough to keep local goods yards open when all the other traffic dropped off. The goods shed visible in this photo is a standard GNSR design in wood with corrugated iron roof. Assuming the wooden one shown in the plan above was actually built, this must have been a later replacement.

(Sandy Murdoch)

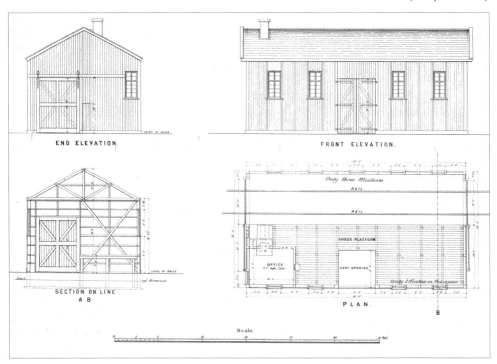

Formartine and Buchan Railway Drawing for Mintlaw Goods Shed. Unfortunately it is undated but the style matches other sheds on the line.   (GNSRA collection)

The station building at Mintlaw as it was in 1994, after restoration for potential business use but before being destroyed by fire. This is the view from the station approach, with the platform just visible on the left. The characteristic stone building style is evident, although Mintlaw benefited from a larger building than most stations on the line. (Keith Fenwick)

After Mintlaw, the line passed under the Fraserburgh road just north of Mintlaw village and continued on fairly level ground to Longside (32¼ miles) which had a neat building on the Peterhead bound platform and for a short period during and after World War I was the junction for the short line to Lenabo Airship Station.

Two small stations followed. Newseat (34 miles) had a two-storey combined

Looking west at Longside in the 1950s. The road to the village can be seen in the distance on the left. The goods yard was on the right and the Lenabo branch went off to the left behind the photographer. (Colin Brown)

Newseat was a square two-storey building quite unlike any others on the line except Mormond. It still had the Great North's characteristic small panes of coloured glass in the windows. Seen here in the 1950s the top floor still appears to have been in use as a dwelling house. After a period of dereliction it was rebuilt as a house in 1989.   (John Emslie/GNSRA)

station house and agent's dwelling house. At Inverugie (36 miles), the station house was a later addition in a much more decorative architectural style. A short siding was also provided.

The line then ran on to the terminus at Peterhead (38 miles). The was sited at the north side of the town; on opening a bus was advertised to run from the Horse Bazaar in Lodge Walk via The Inn to meet all trains.

The *Peterhead Sentinel* of 4th July 1862 gave a description of the station, noting that it was originally intended to be temporary until a larger and more permanent one near the harbour was built; clearly plans changed. Details are also shown on the accompanying OS map. A single platform upwards of 500 feet long was provided with a run-round loop. The building was divided into luggage room, guards' room and closet,

The station building at Inverugie was constructed with more architectural embellishment than other stations on the line. The building was left to decay and demolished after being roofless for some time. There was a small goods yard on the Peterhead side to the right and a small signal box on the platform which was originally built to control the siding points but survived until the 1960s as a store.   (John Emslie)

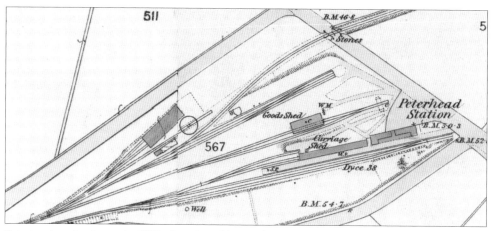

Peterhead station layout in 1868, after the addition of the harbour branch. The layout of the station building is shown below on an 1872 town plan.

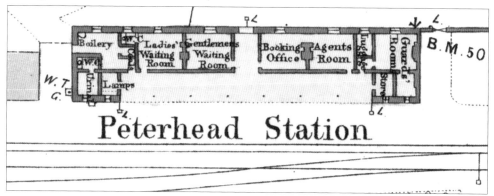

store, stationmaster's room, ticket office, gentlemen's waiting room, ladies' waiting room, boiler room, lamp room and water closets. The mason work of the station was executed by Mr A Stewart, Peterhead, the carpenter work by Mr Laing, Old Deer, the slater work by Mr Kirkton, Peterhead and the plumber work by Messrs Blaikie and Sons of Aberdeen.

Next to the station was the carriage shed, a long and somewhat unshapely wooden building to hold spare carriages. On the north of that there was an extensive goods yard with engine shed, water tower and turntable. Water for the locomotives originally came from Howe O'Buchan, forced up by two powerful "rams" to the top of the brae on the old road overlooking Blackhowe to give it sufficient fall. These were the design and work of Mr White, coppersmith, Peterhead,

Unlike the intermediate stations on the line, the passenger facilities were improved over the years. The eastern end of the platform was enclosed, no doubt to the relief of all concerned. The carriage shed was removed and a second platform face constructed. The platform awning was another later addition. When the loop by the platform was used for van traffic, trains had to reverse out of the platform for the coaches to be gravity shunted to release the loco.

The Harbour branch led off from the north side of the goods yard, crossed the Fraserburgh road on the level and ran round the north side of the town to reach the harbour, a distance of over a mile. Connection was made with tram rails laid along the quay by the Harbour Trustees. The principal traffic would have been fish although some general merchandise would have been carried. With the increasing

The exterior of the station the 1950s. The road to the town runs off to the left. The original station building shown has been enlarged with a new section of roof and an awning over the road entrance. The original roof is apparent on the right. The train shed has a dressed granite wall next to the road. A Scammell Scarab mechanical horse waits to deliver parcels in the town.   (John Emslie/GNSRA)

use of the harbour due to its continued development the tram rails became a nuisance to efficient working of the quays and were gradually abandoned. Then in the 1890s the harbour itself was considerably enlarged and the branch shortened by nearly 400 yards. When motor lorries became common, it was as easy to move goods to and from the station as it was to the branch terminal; consequently by the Second World War the branch had fallen into disuse, although the rails were not finally lifted until after nationalisation.

While stations with overall roofs gave passengers protection against the weather, the interior could be quite gloomy. At Peterhead there were at least roof lights to brighten the place as this view in September 1962 shows. The iron roof supports on the left are of note.   (G N Turnbull/GNSRA)

Peterhead station spread over a wide area to the north of the passenger platforms which are straight ahead. The sidings were in the middle with the locomotive shed on the left - that was larger than the one at Fraserburgh and not fully used. (John Emslie/GNSRA)

By May 1969, when this photo of the platforms at Peterhead was taken from the signal post, many fittings had been removed, but the basic features of the station can still be seen. The station building, hidden by the platform awning, was largely in original condition; to its right the shed added over the main platform is visible behind the train. Further right is the run-round loop which had been adapted to handle Crosse & Blackwell traffic by the addition of the corrugated iron awning. The train in the platform is the Association's Formartine & Buchan Railtour. (Mike Yeoman)

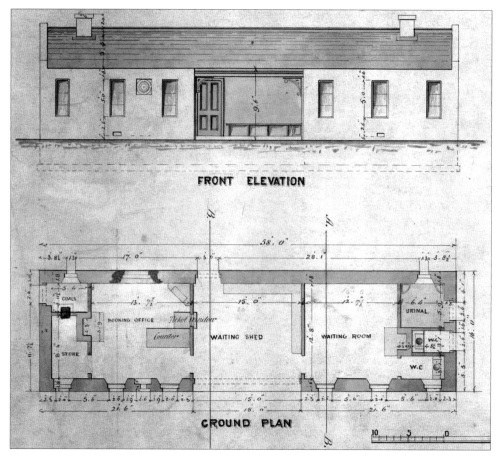

FRONT ELEVATION

GROUND PLAN

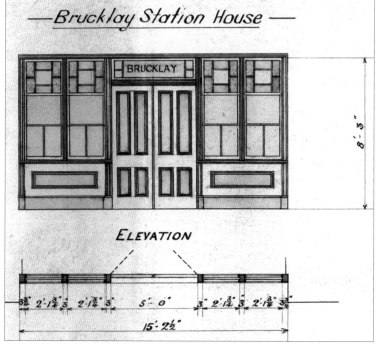

This original plan for the station building at Brucklay shows a typical Buchan line building. The main waiting area was originally open at the front, but was enclosed by a wood and glass wall, shown right. The photograph on the next page shows how little the building changed over the years.
(GNSRA collection)

— Brucklay Station House —

BRUCKLAY

ELEVATION

The Branches Described

Fraserburgh Line

Presumably because the section to Peterhead opened first it was regarded as the main line whereas Maud to Fraserburgh was treated as a branch until BR days, despite the importance of the latter town and the fact that from the railway point of view it always generated more traffic than Peterhead. Brucklay (1¾ miles) was the first station, sited adjacent to the bridge which carried the Mintlaw to New Pitsligo road over the railway. It was close to Brucklay House but otherwise isolated. A crossing loop was provided in 1891.

After heading north through Brucklay, the line now turns eastward in a long arc to pass to the south and east of Strichen (5¾ miles), the only station on the branch to serve a town. This was founded in 1764

The 3 ton capacity crane in the goods yard at Brucklay was typical of those provided at smaller stations. The concrete building in the background was another common sight and would have been installed in the 1950s to store feedstuffs. (John Emslie/GNSRA)

Brucklay from the south end in the 1950s. One signal box was sufficient here and at the other Fraserburgh line stations.   (John Emslie/GNSRA)

(Above) The line crossed the North Ugie Water by a three span viaduct to the south of the town. Seen in 2004, this survives as part of the Formartine & Buchan Way. (Keith Fenwick)

(Right) Station staff grouped in front of the signal box. Cap badges read "GNSR" and the dress and hair styles suggest post First World War. The stationmaster is standing on the right. (Ross Kerby collection)

Strichen from the south end, November 1964. The tablet catcher stand can be seen in the right foreground. (Norris Forrest)

by Lord Strichen, whose descendants were responsible for giving nearby Mormond Hill its White Horse and White Stag, both turf cutouts filled with quartz. The station was on the east edge of the town.

Mormond (8¼ miles) was a small wayside station, never very busy so much so that it was considered for closure as early as 1890 when the owner of the Stationmaster's house declined to renew the lease. Later a two storey station house was constructed, similar to that at Newseat.

Mormond looking north in the 1950s. This was another isolated station which never generated much traffic and had a meagre train service. There was a short siding at the south end. (Colin Brown)

Lonmay looking towards Fraserburgh one evening in the 1950s. The goods shed, part of a small goods yard, can be seen between the station building and the signal box. As was usual, a small wooden waiting room was provided on the opposite platform; this was a later addition.   (John Emslie/GNSRA)

The line continued in a generally easterly direction to Lonmay (10¾ miles), the last crossing point on the branch, before turning north towards Fraserburgh. Rathen (13¼ miles) was like the previous two stations, in a rural setting. It had a single platform and small goods yard. The village was about 1½ miles away and just as close to Lonmay station.

The final intermediate station was

Rathen station building, with the line from Maud coming in on the right. To the left of the building is the signal box installed in 1894 but only in use for a short time as it was found not to be necessary. The building survived in use as a store.   (Colin Brown)

An Up train passing Philorth in July 1950 hauled by class D41 No. 62230. The building here was smaller but had been enlarged with wooden gable roofed extension.   (G H Robin/GNSRA collection)

The approach to Fraserburgh station in 1898, before the station had been enlarged, taken from the Dalrymple Hall. The roof of the engine shed can be seen in the foreground with track to the passenger shed to its left. The locomotive appears to have reversed its coaches out of the platform and is running round. Long lines of goods wagons can be seen in sidings beyond the road bridge; they could be coal wagons to fuel the trawlers.   (GNSRA collection)

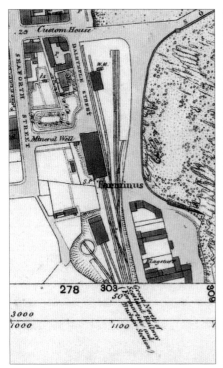

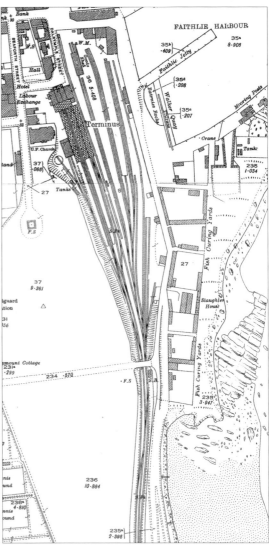

(Above) The original layout at Fraserburgh is shown on this extract from a town plan of 1869. The harbour is at the top. The 1926 OS map on the right shows how the station and harbour were enlarged in the early years of the twentieth century.

Philorth (14½ miles) which until June 1926 was a private station for Lord Saltoun and could be used only by those who had his written permission to do so.

At Fraserburgh, known to one and all as "the Broch" (16 miles from Maud and 41 miles from Dyce) the terminus was alongside the harbour. The original station facilities here included a train shed and single platform as illustrated on page 18. The station was completely rebuilt in granite to cater for the opening of the St. Combs branch with three platforms and substantial awnings. The original engine shed, to the west of the station, survived the rebuilding and, much changed, is still in commercial use today. Fish business was always important, mornings being a hive of activity as the vans were loaded

for the dedicated trains which ran south to Aberdeen to be attached to the appropriate Fish Specials for the south. Traffic in the 1950s was sufficient to justify investment in new goods offices; they survive today in local authority use.

The Consolidated Pneumatic Tool Company, better known as the "Toolies", established its works in the late 19th century just to the south of the town and the west of the line and was served by a private siding. For many years fishing was the lifeline of the town, but, as this slowly declined the local economy was helped by the establishment of other industries such as ship repair.

The passenger side of Fraserburgh station in the 1930s. A class F4 sits on the turntable to the right of the water tower. The locomotive shed is tucked in beside the platforms, which are long enough for any trains likely to use the line. On the right hand platform, under the awning, stand the coaches for the St. Combs train, a motley collection of six wheelers. The town lies beyond the station, dominated by the United Free Church on the left and Dalrymple Hall in the middle distance. (LGRP/GNSRA collection)

The fish loading platform at Fraserburgh. Fish has been brought up from the market hall on lorries which are unloading into the wagons on the right. In the distance is the goods office built in the early 1950s. Another train is also being loaded, with the help of a mobile crane. An old coach body on the left provides storage or shelter for the workers. The photographer had a summer job at Fraserburgh and reeked of fish at the end of the day. (John Emslie/GNSRA)

A good vantage point at Fraserburgh was the embankment on the west side of the station. In the mid-1950s, Ivatt 2-6-0 No. 46460, fitted with a cowcatcher for the St. Combs line, shunts as a 2-6-4T departs on a train for Maud. This includes several fish vans.   (Sandy Murdoch)

A St. Combs train runs into Fraserburgh in the early 1950s. Ex-GER F4 No.67151 leads an LNER 6-wheel full brake and then three ex-GNSR saloon coaches, two of which are those converted from the steam railcars. Saloon stock was preferred on the St. Combs branch as the guard could issue tickets for the unstaffed halts. The length of the train is testimony to the popularity of this branch at a time when the lines to Aberdeen were being used less and less.   (Sandy Murdoch)

The north facing street entrance to the station showed interesting architectural details including crow-stepped walls and large windows. (Colin Brown)

Local delivery of parcels and goods was always important but often carried out by independent operators. With increasing competition, the railway took more direct control and employed a considerable number of lorry drivers. Goods were carried to the nearest station by rail, then collected by lorry for delivery. Quite a large mileage could be involved in an area such as Buchan. Road travel was not without its dangers, so to encourage road safety and minimise the risk of damage to goods, certificates were awarded annually to accident-free drivers. Driver John Howatt and colleagues are shown receiving certificates at Fraserburgh in early BR days. (Courtesy Mrs Roselyn Yule)

Cairnbulg station with its small goods yard to the left. The level crossing beyond the platform marked the boundary between Cairnbulg and Inverallochy in the distance.   (Colin Brown)

St Combs Branch

The St. Combs trains used the east side platform at Fraserburgh and ran south parallel to the Maud line for about half a mile. Few earthworks were needed as for the most part the track was laid more or less on the surface even though this led

From the Minutes of the Finance Committee, 3 September 1865

The Master of Saltoun claimed £36.15/- for three boxes of cigars consigned to him and totally destroyed by being run over by the 12 noon ex-Fraserburgh on 27th July, the brakesman of that train having dropped it from his van while passing Philorth Station. To be settled on best possible terms.

View from rear the cab on 24th April 1965 of the branch diesel unit on its way between Fraserburgh, which can be seen in the distance, and St. Combs. It is clear to see why cowcatchers were originally required on this unfenced line. The competing bus only ran as far as Cairnbulg and Inverallochy as the road to St. Combs was poor.   (J L Stevenson, courtesy Hamish Stevenson)

The branch train at St. Combs waiting to return to Fraserburgh hauled by a J90 (GNSR Class D) 0-6-0T fitted with cowcatchers at both ends. Despite being in LNER days, the coaches are all Great North 6 wheelers – a Cowan-design brake and two Manson Thirds. (GNSRA collection)

to many rapid changes of gradient, some as steep as 1 in 50. Being a light railway, with speed limited to 25mph there was no fencing and as it was worked on the basis of only one engine in steam, there were no signals, although the driver had to hold the single line token. This led to a rather strange instruction being sent to the Station Masters at Cairnbulg and St. Combs. In the event of an engine failure they were to send a Post Office telegram to their counterpart at Fraserburgh asking for a relief engine to be

St. Combs looking towards the buffer stops in the 1950s. The houses lay between the station and the sea. The sidings are empty, although some freight was handled such as fertilisers and, in season, seed potatoes. One of the trains ran as a mixed to convey the freight traffic. After the goods facilities and station staff were withdrawn in 1960, the building was demolished, leaving just an old van body as protection for waiting passengers. (John Emslie/GNSRA)

Auchmacoy appears to have eluded photographers but Pitlurg featured on this postcard which was posted on 15th August 1904 showing an Ellon bound train departing. As with Auchmacoy, there were few houses in the area.   (GNSRA collection)

sent. As the token was still with the driver of the failed engine the telegram itself became the authority to enter the branch without the token. Clearly the railway company had great faith in the GPO telegram service.

The lack of fences meant that the engine had to be equipped with a cow-catcher and this continued into BR days. When diesel railcars arrived this was not possible, presumably because they were too heavy for the light railcars.

When the line opened there was a small platform at Philorth Bridge (2¼ miles), the first station being at Inverallochy (3½ miles) although within weeks the name had been altered to Cairnbulg, before reaching the terminus at St. Combs (5 miles). About a year later a further platform was opened at Kirkton Bridge (1 mile), on the outskirts of Fraserburgh. The two platforms were request stops only; photographic evidence suggest that Kirkton Bridge never had any form of shelter while an old coach body did duty at Philorth Bridge. Both Cairnbulg and St. Combs had small wooden buildings to accommodate staff and waiting passengers and had limited siding facilities.

Cruden Section

The Cruden branch left the line at Ellon and ran around the north side of the town to head towards Cruden Bay. Substantial wooden station houses in contemporary style were constructed at all the stations. Auchmacoy (3¼ miles) and Pitlurg (5½ miles), which had a passing loop and two platforms, were both fairly isolated stations but Hatton (8¼ miles) at least served the village of the same name.

The principal intermediate station was Cruden Bay (10¼ miles) which had two platforms and a much larger station building, as befitted its status in serving the hotel. There was a Refreshment Room on the Up platform while the platforms themselves were protected by ornate iron and glass canopies – unheard of on most other Great North country stations. All this came to an end in April 1931 while re-painting was in progress when a blow-lamp set fire to adjoining woodwork. The blaze quickly spread and the Up side buildings were totally destroyed. The paucity of traffic meant that re-building was not worthwhile; instead all trains used the Down platform and the passing loop, together with that at

The last building on the branch to survive was the goods shed at Hatton, seen here in 2004, but it was demolished in 2009. It is a standard Great North wooden hipped-roof design. (Keith Fenwick)

Pitlurg, was removed the following January.

A siding (11 miles) served the Cruden Bay Brick and Tile Works after which there was a halt at Bullers O'Buchan (12 miles) opened in 1899 principally to allow visitors to see the spectacular cliff scenery. Longhaven (13½ miles), serving a few houses, was reached before the terminus at Boddam (15¼ miles). As well as the usual facilities a large corrugated iron clad

Although of indifferent quality, this postcard does show the ample facilities provided at Cruden Bay. The main building is on the Up platform, with the signal box next to it. The Down platform has a substantial waiting room, far larger than would ever be needed as few passengers would have boarded a Down train. Both platforms have generous awnings. (Ross Kerby/GNSRA)

Cruden Bay in June 1937 after fire had destroyed the main building on the Up platform and the passenger service had been withdrawn. The hotel tramway can be seen in the centre with the goods shed on the right.
(GNSRA collection)

carriage shed was built here which survived until at least the 1930s, when it looked as though the next strong easterly wind would bring the whole thing down.

Cruden Bay Hotel lay about a mile from the station so to ease access for visitors a narrow gauge electric railway connected them, the current being generated at the hotel's power house with services operated by two 4-wheeled trams. After the branch passenger services were withdrawn in October 1932 access to the hotel became a problem so in 1934 the LNER purchased a large Rolls-Royce car to convey guests from Aberdeen station. On the outbreak of war in 1939 the hotel closed and was requisitioned by the War Office, although the laundry and boiler house remained in railway ownership until March 1942. After the War, attempts were made to sell the hotel but there was no interest. It was never re-opened and was eventually demolished. The tramway

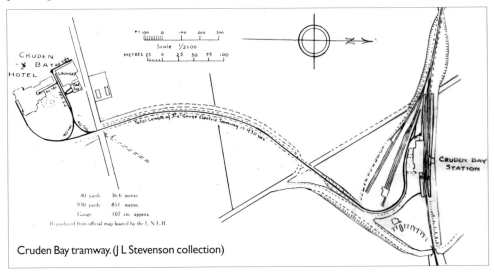

Cruden Bay tramway. (J L Stevenson collection)

This postcard of the village of Boddam shows the railway line running towards the terminus on the top left. The village was quite scattered and did not offer the prospect of significant traffic to the branch line. An extension to Peterhead would have been relatively cheap but would have had a negative affect on overall revenue. (GNSRA collection)

finally closed in March 1941. The wooden Club House on the golf course survives, complete with Great North coloured glass in a few windows.

Both tram bodies survived as summer houses and one was later restored to its former glory and can now be seen in the Grampian Transport Museum at Alford, attached to a replacement chassis but not operational.

The Boddam line was constructed on a substantial scale, typified by the solid stone construction of this bridge to the east of Cruden Bay which still stands. (Keith Fenwick)

The original passenger service showed five return services to Boddam each day but these were gradually reduced until only two remained at the end. Trains were normally allowed about 35 minutes for the journey. As befitted a rural branch line most inwards freight would have related to the agricultural nature of the surrounding countryside along with coal supplies for the district. Both the Cruden Bay Brick & Tile Works and Longhaven Quarry had private sidings which helped to generate outwards traffic but the expected fish loadings from Boddam never reached expectations.

Over the years the worst fears expressed by the Board regarding viability proved well founded. When in 1903 the Company carried out a detailed examination of the costs of the various branch lines, the Cruden Section showed the poorest results of them all by a considerable measure.

Despite repeated requests by the citizens of Peterhead for the 3 mile gap to Boddam be filled in, thus giving them a shorter journey to Aberdeen, the Board consistently turned them down no doubt because the reduced mileage would have meant less income for the Company and put traffic via Maud at risk. Even as late as 1927, the LNER Scottish General Manager raised the question with the Traffic Superintendent at Aberdeen but the latter was unenthusiastic to say the least and the matter was finally dropped.

In October 1932 Passenger services were suspended for the Winter months and all timetables were marked to this effect. Services were never resumed and in June 1933 passenger trains were officially withdrawn, the last train having run on Saturday 29th October 1932. There were no long drawn out inquiries in those days. Freight trains were withdrawn from 7th November 1945 following which the section north of Cruden Bay was closed completely

However there was one final use for the branch. At the end of the war large numbers of goods wagons needed repair or scrapping at various works. Somewhere had to be found to store them and those destined for Inverurie were accommodated along the Cruden line. The track was lifted during the latter half of 1950, thus ending a rather unfortunate venture.

A group of staff posed in front of one of the Cruden Bay trams at Cruden Bay station while two women sit patiently waiting inside the tram to set off.   (J L Stevenson/ courtesy Hamish Stevenson)

SIGNALLING

Signalling in the early days was primitive and traffic was controlled by the timetable which clearly showed where trains were due to cross. Any deviation had to be authorized by telegraph from Aberdeen; the Great North had adopted the single needle telegraph from the beginning and used it to safely operate the railway for many years. The fact that the GNSR with around 300 miles of track, most of it single, had only one example of a head-on collision, or "cornfield meet" in American parlance, speaks volumes for the disciplined application by staff of the signalling rules and regulations.

Only a limited number of crossing places was provided initially, but this was gradually increased to match rising traffic levels. Signalling generally consisted of distant (originally distance) signals to stop trains outside the stations and a double armed station signal in the middle of the station to control departures.

Resignalling took place at Maud in the period 1880-81 to improve the handling of trains there and this appears to be the first instance of full interlocking of points and signals on the line. The cost was estimated to be £1,171 in 1880 and this matches the provision of the two signal boxes.

Little else changed until the 1889 Regulation of Railways Act required all passenger carrying routes to be worked by the block system with the added protection on single lines of giving the driver clear authority to proceed. The Act also required that points and signals be interlocked. Conformation with these requirements placed a heavy financial burden on the Great North and implementation took several years to complete. However the busy Buchan line was one of the first to be converted, by August 1894.

Tyer's No. 6 Electric Tablet, which

At Dyce, a separate box was provided where the single line started just north of the station to control the points there and exchange tokens. Its functions were taken over by the South box in 1928, but the building still stood in 1962 as it was used by the foreman of the adjacent Engineer's yard. (Norris Forrest)

The signalman at Auchnagatt was happy to be photographed in the 1950s. This box design was used at most stations on the Buchan lines except for the Cruden section.   (John Emslie/GNSRA)

was regarded as 'state of the art', was employed to ensure that only one train was on each single line section at a time. At the beginning of the 20th century, there were crossing loops at Newmachar, Udny, Ellon, Arnage, Auchnagatt, Maud, Brucklay, Strichen, Lonmay, Mintlaw and Longside to accommodate the traffic.

Because of the dangers of exchanging tablets at speed, automatic exchange apparatus was later developed and installed at all the crossing points on the lines to Fraserburgh and Peterhead. The familiar tablet catcher can be seen in many photographs of signal boxes and locomotives. In the early 1930s, long section working was introduced between Maud and both Strichen and Longside as an economy measure so that Brucklay and Mintlaw boxes could close at night.

After installation of full interlocking, typical signalling at each station consisted of distant, home and starting signals for each direction. At Newmachar, Udny, Ellon, Auchnagatt, Maud and Mintlaw two signal boxes were needed because there was a limit to the distance between signal box and points. One box was configured to control the signals and accommodated the tablet instruments while the other box was really an elevated ground frame. Even so, some of these minor boxes were equipped with fire places which could hardly ever have been used.

At the other crossing loops, one signal box sufficed. Initially signal boxes and token instruments were also provided at non-crossing stations to operate siding points. However, after only a few months it was realised that this was excessive and the token instruments were taken out. A ground frame was provided, released by the tablet for the relevant section.

At Maud, the larger layout required two signal boxes, a south box on the Down side to control the junction and access to the sidings and a north box just north of the station house and adjacent to the Fraserburgh line to control the lines towards Fraserburgh and Peterhead with double block line working between them; in 1935, the LNER replaced these with one signal box at the south end of the Peterhead Up platform.

One change during the 1920s was the introduction of long section working to enable the signal boxes at Brucklay and Mintlaw to be switched out when traffic was quiet. An additional pair of token instruments had to be provided for the long section.

Another change at that time was the replacement of some tablet instruments by Tyer's Key Token instruments. By having alternate sections as tablet and key token, drivers were more likely to realise if they had the wrong authorisation for the section.

The block sections ranged in length from 1 mile 1745 yards between Maud and Brucklay to 5 miles 1159 yards between Longside and Peterhead, but the ruling section in terms of time was that between Dyce and Newmachar which required 20 minutes for an unfitted goods train to toil up the 1 in 75 gradient from Dyce. By 1914 it had become clear that the line was at or near capacity so in the following year an Act was obtained permitting construction of double track from Dyce to Ellon. Only a short section, between Parkhill and Elrick signal box, a distance of 1 mile 1197 yards was converted and this was opened on 20th

May 1920, closed on 2nd October 1921 and then used seasonally during the height of the fishing season, being finally closed on 23rd August 1925, after which the second track was lifted. A loop was also provided at Esslemont and used when the double line was in operation.

It has to be said that the benefits of the doubling must have been called into question by drivers trying to restart heavy, loose coupled trains stopped at Elrick when crossing. And in case an Up train could not stop on the falling gradient, Parkhill was prohibited from accepting a train from Elrick when one was signalled from Dyce; the Up train had to wait at Elrick until the Down train had entered the double track section.

It might be thought that the provision of passing places was generous, but this is not so when the peak traffic is considered. It was necessary to operate the traffic in flights of trains, based around the daily southbound fish traffic, and to extend the opening hours of signal boxes.

In the summer of 1948, for example, the first 5 trains of the day, all Goods trains from Kittybrewster at 3.15 and 3.50am to Fraserburgh, 3.35 and 4.15am to Peterhead

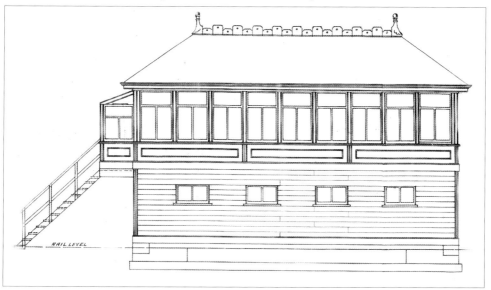

The construction of the St. Combs branch required a new signal box at Fraserburgh, opened in August 1904 when it replaced one from ten years earlier. This wooden design showed some of the features of contemporary wooden station buildings. (GNSRA collection)

and 5.00am to Ellon, had to make only two crossings between them to reach their destinations. By the time that the fish trains had started to flow southwards with the 9.46am from Fraserburgh, the majority of the Down goods trains had reached their destinations thus minimising the number of time consuming crossings and potential delays from late running trains in the opposite direction. Likewise most of the slower moving Up goods trains were started after the fish trains; indeed the final two such trains of the day from Peterhead and Fraserburgh did not reach Kittybrewster until 10.30 and 11.50pm respectively.

The 12.50pm Goods from Kittybrewster to Fraserburgh was an exception and had a very slow journey. After crossing Up trains at Dyce, Udny and Arnage, it crossed three at Auchnagatt, where it waited from 3.06pm until 3.58pm, and another one at Maud. At Strichen it sat from 5.12pm until 5.54pm waiting to be overtaken by the 4.00pm passenger from Aberdeen.

Few changes were made to the signalling until the 1960s. Gradually lower quadrant arms were replaced by LNER or BR upper quadrant ones. Declining traffic in the 1960s and the closure of goods sidings allowed some of the block posts to be dispensed with before closure to passenger services. After that, telephone working was used for the section from Dyce to Maud, and the

Drivers had to be able to recognise signals from a distance. This set of signals at the site of Elrick box was set up in the 1950s to do just that. The hut contained their controls.(GNSRA collection)

sections on from there to both Fraserburgh and Peterhead were operated under One Engine in Steam regulations. This enabled two goods services to operate daily. In later years, the whole line was worked as a single section.

The signalman had quite a distance to walk at Maud to exchange tokens with the driver of this Fraserburgh bound train on 1st March 1965. The process took much longer when trains crossed.

(Sandy Murdoch)

Train Services

Passenger services varied little and after the early days consisted of a very basic service of 5 or 6 trains each way per day. Average speeds, including the many stops, of around 30mph did little to encourage passenger custom and it is hardly surprising that what the local populace knew as the "Buchan trainie" became something of a butt for their jokes, albeit usually of the affectionate variety. In truth the service was a humdrum affair which never escaped from its Victorian antecedents. The 1923 timetable even includes a separate table for the journey between Peterhead and Fraserburgh, with connection times at Maud ranging from a few minutes to nearly 2 hours.

The mainstay of the route, however, was the fish traffic from the ports of Peterhead and Fraserburgh and the general goods and livestock business generated by these stations and on the branch as a whole. The table below gives an indication of traffic density over the years as measured by the total numbers of trains (those splitting and/or combining at Maud are counted as single ones) of each category. Some of the figures are estimates.

There were also some shorter workings, for instance only as far as Ellon, and during

Number of trains over the years

	1863	1893	1907	1922	1930	1948	1960
Passenger	8	10	13	10	10	10	10
Fish	-	3	5	5	6	7	2
Goods	2	11	8	11	7	15	8
Total	10	24	26	26	23	32	20

Arrivals and departures could be occasions for many locals to turn out but crowds such as this were reserved for special events, in this case the departure of Miss Henderson from Maud on 21st October 1912. She had been a teacher at Maud public school for many years and was going to South Africa to be married. She was given a hearty send off by pupils and friends.   (Ross Kerby collection)

the 1920s, some trains ran as combined passenger and fish from Fraserburgh and Peterhead to Maud, then as separate trains for each type of traffic.

The number of timetabled trains peaked in 1948, but all the figures should be taken with some reserve given that a significant proportion of fish and livestock traffic was worked as short notice special trains. It is fortunate that some, but by no means all, of the records for 1948 have survived, but even then these do not include the ad-hoc trains arranged by the Aberdeen District Control. They do, however, allow a reasonably detailed look at the planned operations for the summer of that year.

In 1948 there were roundly 16 trains each way, excluding those operated on limited days and other "odd" workings. The passenger service in 1948 followed the time honoured pattern of 5 trains each way, with separate portions for Peterhead and Fraserburgh splitting or combining at Maud depending on the direction of travel. Each portion was composed of 2 passenger coaches, 1 composite and 1 third, and a full bogie brake van, giving a total of 6 vehicles to be hauled on the Aberdeen - Maud part of the journey. To maintain the service 18 elderly vehicles, mainly of GNSR and NER origins, were required but trains were often more heavily loaded than the modest numbers of diagrammed vehicles suggested.

The commonest additional vehicles on Down trains were horseboxes and special cattle vans carrying newly weaned calves from the dairy farming areas of the English West Country to Maud for conversion into finest Aberdeenshire beef. The capacity of the bogie brake vans was quite often inadequate to cope with orthodox parcels traffic and additional vehicles had to be attached as the need arose. It would be easy to underestimate the variety and volume of the goods with which the guards had to deal. Apart from the staples of GPO parcels and mails and the railways' own miscellaneous parcels business there could be found day old chicks in boxes, dogs on

Near Maud on 11th August 1950, LMS 2P No. 622 heads a typical mixed freight. By then the loco should have carried its BR number, 40622, but it had not even been branded BRITISH RAILWAYS. There is quite a mixture of wagons on the train; most are covered vans, but there are a couple of open wagons, one low sided, an oil tank wagon, a flat with container and a long wheelbase van. Thirty years before, most of the wagons would have been open ones.   (Sandy Murdoch)

The working of heavy southbound fish specials resulted in extra engines having to work north. Rather than do so light engine, they would be attached to service trains, such as this Peterhead bound one setting off from Maud in May 1949. In the background can be seen a Great North wooden footbridge. It was replaced a few months later by a metal one using old rails. (Sandy Murdoch)

B12 No. 61511 hauls an Up passenger train near Maud. The train is made up of three ex-Great North vehicles, including a full brake, with a long-wheelbase 4-wheeled van tacked on the rear. (Sandy Murdoch)

BI No.61348 shunts cattle wagons on 30th August 1950. The loco was built at Gorton, Manchester, and put into traffic at Kittybrewster in June 1949. It is painted in LNER apple green but with BRITISH RAILWAYS on the tender.   (Sandy Murdoch)

leads, dogs and other animals in boxes, calves in sacks, pigs in crates, fish in boxes; the list was endless. Motor bikes, push bikes, prams, spares for farm machinery and for marine engines; in fact just about everything conceivable. In season extra vehicles could be required for hampers of dead game and poultry for Smithfield and other meat markets throughout the country.

The introduction of diesel multiple unit trains in the early 1960s, with their limited van capacity and their inability to haul additional vans, led to the ludicrous situation of separate parcels trains having to be operated. This, of course, negated the hoped for economies stemming from the replacement of steam hauled trains by diesel units and several workings reverted to locomotive haulage. This in turn meant that the splitting and combining of trains at Maud was abandoned and Peterhead passengers usually had to change trains.

For the first few years after nationalisation the railways still carried the bulk of the nation's freight including large quantities of "Sundries" or traffic in small consignments of less than a ton. Such traffic moved in astonishing quantity and variety by means of a network of daily vans and a sorting system not unlike the present Royal Mail post codes. Peterhead and Fraserburgh would have probably received daily vans of sundries from Aberdeen, Dundee, Glasgow and Edinburgh. On most days there would have been vans from places further afield such as Newcastle, Birmingham and others of the now forgotten large goods stations through which most consumer goods passed for distribution round the country. All this was in addition to traffic in bulk ranging from coal to flour. Similar commodities passed to the smaller stations on the Buchan lines although, of course, in lesser quantities and places such as Udny, Ellon, Maud and Mintlaw which served wide hinterlands handled a great variety of traffic.

The Buchan area having some of the

finest farmland worked by some of the most progressive farmers in Scotland, it goes without saying that the line received large quantities of agricultural traffic including animal feeding stuffs, fertilisers, and draff from the Speyside distilleries. There were smaller items such as bales of fencing wire, drums of sheep dip, and machinery spares. The main outwards products were seed oats and seed potatoes, not forgetting the containers of eggs from the Egg Packing Station at Ellon. The most audible travellers on the line were, without doubt, the livestock from the Marts at Ellon, Maud and Strichen. Maud was the main centre with three Marts and was reputed to process more fat cattle than any other market town in the UK. Much of the livestock, like the fish traffic, was moved by special trains and to give only a single example seven such trains were operated between Monday 5th and Thursday 9th September, 1948. The trains were from Strichen (2), Maud (3) and Ellon (2) and conveyed between

them a grand total of 1,105 cattle, 585 sheep and 62 pigs to destinations as diverse as Dyce, Kittybrewster, Arbroath, Dundee, St. Andrews, Buckhaven, Kirkcaldy, Glasgow, Newcastle, York, Leeds, Hull, Liverpool and Manchester.

As with the fish trains the livestock specials were worked by Kittybrewster enginemen and guards. The usual practice was to attach engines and vans to Down trains from Kittybrewster, or to use them to work ad-hoc specials. The instructions for just one train extracted from a Supplementary Weekly Circular give a good example of how it was done - "Thursday 9 September (1948) : B12 engine (tender first) and brakevan. Assist 8.43am Goods Kittybrewster to Fraserburgh to Maud. Thence Engine and Van to Strichen. Shunt. Work 2.00pm No. 2 Express Goods Special Strichen to Guild Street."

The trains on the Buchan lines were worked in the main from the Aberdeen end. There were, to be sure, three engines

D8616 shunts at Peterhead in the 1960s. By then, the use of open wagons had all but ceased in favour of covered vans. The passenger platforms are to the right. The loco shed stood for several years after it was taken out of use. The Class 14 Claytons were not a successful design and are not recorded as having been allocated to either depot in Aberdeen so this may have been a trial working.   (Sandy Murdoch)

Y 284 X

Strichen, Lonmay, &c., Holiday
MONDAY, 1st AUGUST

DAY EXCURSION TO ABERDEEN

OUTWARD JOURNEY			One-Day Third Class Return Fare	RETURN JOURNEY		
	a.m.	a.m.	s. d.		p.m.	p.m.
Rathen ... ...dep.	7.29	9.12	} 3 8	Aberdeen ... ...dep.	4.30	7. 0
Lonmay ... ... „	7.35	9.17		Strichen ... ...arr.	6. 1	8.36
Mormond ... ... „	7.41	...		Mormond ... ... „	...	8.42
Strichen ... ... „	7.47	9.26		Lonmay ... ... „	6.10	8.47
Aberdeen ... ...arr.	9.27	10.45		Rathen ... ... „	6.15	8.52

SPECIAL CHEAP FARES—All Trains

From LONMAY TO	Third Single	Seven Day Third Return	From RATHEN TO	Third Single	Seven Day Third Return
	s. d.	s. d.		s. d.	s. d.
Aberdeen	3 2	4 9	Aberdeen	3 2	4 9
Bucksburn	3 2	4 2	Bucksburn	3 2	4 6
Cairnbulg	...	1 5	Dyce	3 2	4 2
Dyce	3 2	4 2	Ellon	...	3 2
Ellon	...	2 8	Fraserburgh	...	0 5½
Fraserburgh	...	0 9½	Kittybrewster...	3 2	4 9
Inverugie	...	2 1	Maud	...	1 7
Kittybrewster	3 2	4 9			
Maud	...	1 6			
Peterhead	...	2 1			
St Combs	...	1 8			

From MORMOND TO	Third Single	Seven Day Third Return	From STRICHEN TO	Third Single	Seven Day Third Return
	s. d.	s. d.		s. d.	s. d.
Aberdeen	3 2	4 2	Aberdeen	3 2	4 2
Bucksburn	3 2	3 11	Arnage	...	1 7
Cairnbulg	...	1 8	Auchnagatt...	...	1 5
Dyce	3 2	3 8	Bucksburn	3 2	3 8
Fraserburgh	...	1 1	Cairnbulg	1 1	2 0
Kittybrewster...	3 2	4 2	Dyce	3 2	3 8
Maud	...	1 2	Ellon	1 7	2 1
St Combs	...	1 11	Fraserburgh	0 9½	1 5
			Inverugie	...	2 1
			Kittybrewster	3 2	4 2
			Maud	...	0 9½
			Mintlaw	...	1 7
			Newmachar	...	2 11
			Peterhead	...	2 1
			Udny	...	2 11

CONDITIONS OF ISSUE.

Day, Half-day and Evening tickets are issued subject to the conditions applicable to tickets of these descriptions as shown in the Company's Time Tables.

Tickets at reduced fares (other than Day, Half-day and Evening Tickets), are issued subject to the conditions of issue of ordinary passenger tickets, so far as applicable, as shown in the Company's Time Tables.

Children under three years of age, Free; three years and under fourteen, Half Fares. For Luggage Allowances also see Time Tables.

Aberdeen, July, 1938.

L·N·E·R

Henry Munro, Limited, Aberdeen.

N.S. 3222—750

The LNER and BR gave much attention to publicising their services. Railway posters from the period are now much sought after, even if they painted an optimistic picture of the delights of Fraserburgh beach as opposite. Handbills were handed out in large numbers, not only advertising fares as above but also special excursion trains which were run for holidays and theatre performances.

including the St. Combs branch engine stabled overnight at Fraserburgh and one at Peterhead, but these were part of the Kittybrewster allocation. The two sheds were "Subs" of Kittybrewster and supervised locally by "Drivers in Charge" who received a small pay increment and reported to the Shedmaster at Kittybrewster. There were also two guards based at Peterhead and Fraserburgh, and Fraserburgh had two porter guards for the St. Combs trains.

The greater power of the B1s and the BR Standard Class 4 Mixed traffic tank engines reduced the number of locomotives required in the 1950s. Had similar locomotives been available in earlier years the history of the Buchan line might have taken a different turn. The same traffic could have been hauled more cheaply by fewer trains and the resultant line capacity used to improve the passenger service, which languished, amongst other reasons, because line capacity was largely required for the vastly more profitable fish and freight trains.

Apart from the increased loco power,

little attention appears to have been paid to the possibilities of more efficient operation. It would have been perfectly possible, for instance, to have worked the line without an engine shed at Peterhead. All that was required was to time the first Down freight to arrive before the departure of the first Up passenger train and to work the last Up freight by the engine of the last Down passenger service of the day.

When economies had to be made, it was by the simple expedient of withdrawing trains. By 1956, Fraserburgh continued to be served by five trains each way, but Peterhead only had three. The first Peterhead service reached Aberdeen at 10.54am and the last one left there at 4.2pm. An earlier service was later restored, leaving at 6.40am but a later one was only provided on Saturdays. Passengers could reach Peterhead much more quickly by bus, which offered a more frequent and cheaper service. Why pay more to take longer over the journey? Use of the Fraserburgh line remained higher.

Even dieselisation when it came in 1960 was simply a case of substitution

A typical freight in later years. D5070 heads a Peterhead bound train in the mid-1960s at Maud where single line tokens are exchanged beside the signal box. On the right, the automatic tablet exchanger posts are out of use.   (Sandy Murdoch)

The diesel multiple units used on the Buchan lines were mainly Cravens 2-car sets which brought a new standard of comfort and offered excellent views of the line to passengers. Here, one of the units attracts a crowd of onlookers at St. Combs in July 1963. (Norman Turnbull)

of one form of haulage for another. It is hardly surprising that dieselisation in itself, imposed without fresh thinking, was unable to stem the tide of traffic losses and the eventual closure of a line which had served its users well for over a century. By 1962, through working to Peterhead ceased and most of the services were worked by diesel loco and elderly ex-LMS coaches with diesel multiple units for some of the services. Diesel traction saved about 10 minutes on the journey time from Aberdeen to Fraserburgh.

The St. Combs line continued to be well used as there was no competing bus service beyond Cairnbulg due to local road conditions. The St. Combs line was always a self-contained operation. The first timetable showed six return journeys on weekdays although over the years the frequency of the service varied. Eleven trains ran each way in 1956 and by the time of closure this was down to nine trains with an extra on Saturday. Throughout its life trains were allowed 20 minutes for the journey. Trains

initially consisted of two or three coaches worked by a Class D 0-6-0 tank engine but for a short period in 1905/06 the GNSR tried using its steam railcar; it proved no more successful here than it had been elsewhere so was soon withdrawn.

Latterly one of the ubiquitous 2-car diesel railcars worked the service until the line closed on 3rd May 1965. The line was spared the 4-wheeled railbuses which would not have coped with the traffic on offer.

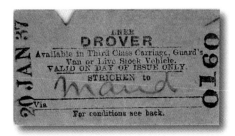

Drover's ticket issued in 1937 for the short journey from Strichen to Maud and valid in Third Class carriage, guard's van or Live Stock vehicle. (Ross Kerby collection)

So much of the freight traffic was seasonal that it was difficult to operate the lines efficiently. Fish landings in particular could vary. Some trains were overloaded while others, such as this fish train near Maud on 2nd June 1950 were uneconomically short. A fitted fish van has been coupled behind the brake van so that it could easily be detached. Class B1 No. 61343 had only been built the previous year. (Sandy Murdoch)

An Up train stands at Ellon in the years before the First World War. It is clearly composed of two portions as there is an open wagon after the third coach which would have been conveying fish. The first vehicle was an outside-framed meat van which could also be used for fish traffic. The locomotive was No. 9, a Class O designed by Manson. In the background lurks No. 11, a Class D 0-6-0T.

(Sir Malcolm Barclay-Harvey/GNSRA collection)

FISH TRAFFIC

Peterhead and Fraserburgh have long been two of Scotland's major fishing ports. The fish traffic generated was an important source of business from GNSR days and was dispatched year round from the Buchan ports but the herring fishing season which lasted from roughly June to September provided the peak forwardings.

The workings in early British Railways days give a good indication of how the traffic was handled. There were three dedicated fish trains daily from Peterhead to Aberdeen and four from Fraserburgh. On Saturdays there was an extra train and an indication of how important the traffic was is shown by the fact that two engines ran light from Aberdeen especially to work it. These trains ran almost as fast as the passenger ones leading to passengers commenting that "Deid fish got a quicker hurl than live passengers."

An interesting feature was the use of insulated containers carried on purpose built flat wagons for traffic from the MacFisheries factory at Fraserburgh to their siding at Finsbury Park, London. Marshalled on the rear of the brake van of the 1.40pm Fish train from Aberdeen to Kings Cross, they could be picked off the train at Finsbury Park with the minimum delay on arrival in London. This was one of a variety of services from Aberdeen via the former LNER and LMS routes by which Buchan line fish traffic was distributed to other parts of the country.

Not all the fish went to Aberdeen in dedicated trains. Many of the passenger trains could have one or more fish vans in their make-up but this useful practice declines when diesel multiple-units ran some of the services as they were not able to have "extras" attached to them.

In 1948 all the fish trains, "Fishers" to the railwaymen, were double headed, largely by B12s and ex-GNSR 4-4-0s. The engines reached the Buchan ports by double heading the first seven trains of the day from Aberdeen, starting with the 3.15am goods to Fraserburgh and finishing with the 8.20am passenger from Aberdeen, all being worked by Kittybrewster crews.

Besides the outward movement of fish traffic from the Buchan ports there was a fairly regular flow of fresh fish from Mallaig to Fraserburgh for processing. This was routed via the connection between the West Highland and Callander & Oban lines at Crianlarich from where it went to Stirling to be attached to the overnight mail from Glasgow to Aberdeen before being worked forward.

Associated with the seasonal herring fishing were the special trains run in the Autumn to Yarmouth and Lowestoft for the benefit of the "Fisher quines" (girls), always "quines" no matter their age, who gutted and packaged the herring. Their travel arrangements were made by the fish curing firms who employed the workers and also paid their fares. They clearly took a good deal of luggage with them as all the trains contained an unspecified number of vans for that purpose.

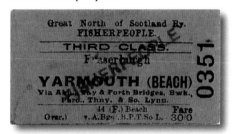

A through Third Class ticket from Fraserburgh to Yarmouth via the East Coast route for fish workers. Other routes were available. (Ross Kerby colln)

LOCOMOTIVES

When the Buchan Line opened trains on the Great North were being worked by small 2-4-0 tender engines built by Messrs. Fairbairn, a well known engineering firm in Manchester. Good enough engines but, especially in winter, the crew would need to be hardy as they lacked even a rudimentary cab until they had been in use for some years. It was not until 1862 that anything larger in the form of 4-4-0s appeared and even these were originally intended for the tortuous railway up Speyside. From then on the Company relied almost entirely on various developments of this type to work its traffic. The final development, itself up-dated from an 1899 design, appeared in 1921 and one of these, No. 49 *Gordon Highlander* has been preserved. Exceptions included a series of 0-4-4 tank engines built primarily for the intensive Aberdeen suburban services but also used on the Cruden Line while No. 8, one of a small series of 0-6-0 tank engines intended mainly for shunting, worked the

(Opposite page) Given its importance to the Great North, just about any class of loco will have appeared on the Buchan lines over the years. The top photograph shows No. 22, a Cowan design of 2-4-0 introduced in 1859 which survived until 1907. Kittybrewster North box is in the background.
(GNSRA collection)

The 4-4-0 in the middle photograph was No. 35 of Class H. It dated from the 1860s and was typical of early 4-4-0s, with outside cylinders and slotted splashers. The cab was quite generous for the day. The 4 wheel tenders allowed the locos to fit on short turntables.   (GNSRA collection)

The bottom photograph shows Class K No. 48A at Kittybrewster in August 1924, not long before it was withdrawn. It had been built in 1866 and was much rebuilt during its life.
(A W Croughton/GNSRA collection)

St. Combs trains. The whole system was beset by severe weight restrictions which prevented the building of larger and more powerful engines. Consequently, as train loads increased, this lack of power led to much double heading.

After the Grouping in 1923 the LNER, in view of these restrictions, was faced with considerable difficulty when it came to replacing older engines as they wore out, especially as the Company had limited cash reserves and the busier areas further south had priority on replacements. The first fresh stock to be brought in were some Class D31s from the North British Railway, themselves hardly in the first flush of youth. In 1931 something much larger arrived from East Anglia in the form of ex-Great Eastern 4-6-0s of Class B12, more powerful and within the weight restrictions although still dating from the years before the 1914 war. Commonly known as "Hikers" they were very different to what the footplate staff were accustomed; however once they settled in they worked well. Over the years, weight restrictions had gradually been eased so that in 1946 the LNER was able to introduce its Class B1 4-6-0, the first brand new engines to arrive in the north-east of Scotland for a quarter of a century.

The St. Combs line needed something very light. In 1926, this was satisfied by importing a North British D51 4-4-0T, followed by three others over the next few years. These, in turn, quickly wore out and were replaced by another import from the Great Eastern, the little 2-4-2 tank engines of Class F4. All were equipped with cow-catchers.

Further changes followed nationalisation on 1st January 1948 since examples of several classes were transferred to

After Manson took over as Locomotive Superintendent in 1884, inside cylinders replaced outside ones. Typical is Class 0, No.7, later LNER Class D42 No.6807, of 1888 which survived until April 1945. Seen at the north end of Kittybrewster.   (GNSRA collection)

Kittybrewster and just about any of them could be rostered. These included former LMS Class 2 4-4-0s. North British J36 0-6-0s and Glen 4-4-0s and Gresley's V4 2-6-2s. Probably the most useful newcomers to Buchan were the BR standard class 4MT 2-6-4 tank engines, commonly known as "Doodlebugs" (locomotive nicknames could form a study in themselves!). These were able to take trains of 300 tons from Peterhead and 290 tons from Fraserburgh, considerably more than most of the older engines, some of which were limited to as little as 120 tons. Clearly much double-heading was eliminated. Other BR standard designs, such as the Class 2MT and Class

With only one locomotive dedicated to operating the St. Combs line, the LNER turned to the ex-North British Railway D51 4-4-0Ts to help out. 10461 was the second to arrive, in July 1927 and is seen here at rest at Kittybrewster. This class dated from the early 1880s, so they were some years older than most of the other engines then operating on the Buchan line. 10461 saw its days out in the north east and was withdrawn in October 1932.   (LGRP)

The ex-Great Eastern F4 2-4-2 tanks were brought to the north east to work the St. Combs line and fitted with cowcatchers fore and aft. No.7164 was photographed at Maud running light engine to Kittybrewster for servicing.
(Sandy Murdoch)

4MT 2-6-0s, also operated.

The early months of 1960 saw the arrival of the diesels in the north-east with Kittybrewster, home to all the Buchan workings, becoming an exclusively diesel depot on 1st July 1961. Thereafter the newcomers reigned supreme. The initial plan was to operate all passenger services by diesel multiple units which would make combining and splitting at Maud much easier. However, passenger trains carried considerable quantities of parcels and urgent goods traffic so locomotive haulage was re-introduced for some workings.

While examples of several classes made their appearance in Buchan the Type 2 built

The Great North tried its steam railcars on the St. Combs branch but they were useless; LNER Sentinel steam railcars proved much more successful, although their use on GNSR lines lasted only from January 1929 to September 1930. They were used between Aberdeen and Ellon, where *Highland Chieftain* was photographed. The way staff are standing suggests this may be a trial run.(Hamish Stevenson collection)

The two Gresley Class V4s spent time at Kittybrewster for a year from August 1954. Here No. 61700 *Bantam Cock* passes Rathen with the former GNSR Royal Saloon on an inspection run.(George Robin)

by the North British Locomotive Company predominated. Notoriously unreliable they gave much grief to traffic operators and did not long survive the closure of Inverurie works in 1969. Kittybrewster shed closed on 14th August 1967 after which the other Aberdeen shed, at Ferryhill, provided the crews. Type 2s, such as Class 27, usually operated the freight services for the remaining years.

A Class 25 heads an Up freight through Auchnagatt on 7th July 1976. Traffic was still healthy at the time with a couple of containers and numerous covered wagons.   (Robin Hogg/GNSRA)

Snow

In the north-east of Scotland, bad weather in winter tends to come from the east. The Buchan Line runs more or less north and south across the lie of the country so that falling snow quickly builds up in the frequent cuttings, however shallow, consequently the line was always liable to be closed. One of the earliest occasions mentioned was when the 5am goods from Aberdeen was de-railed by snow near Newmachar on 12th January 1867, the engine and several wagons falling down an embankment but fortunately the crew was unhurt. The trouble continued as the Minute Book notes that the lines were blocked by snow on 21st and *'The Woman who keeps the level crossing at New Machar had supplied refreshments to passengers'*; no mention that she was re-imbursed.

Snow went on causing problems until the line closed. Two of the worst winters of the 20th century occurred in 1942 and 1947. In the early part of 1942 blizzards closed the line at Newmachar and, further north, between Maud and Brucklay. On 25th January that year the 5am goods from Fraserburgh was trapped in the snow for several days before it was dug out, by which time the engine had almost disappeared. Despite their best efforts railway staff could not cope on their own and the Army had to be called on while an Admiralty trawler was used to deliver mail and other essentials to Peterhead and Fraserburgh.

Winter 1947 was, if anything, even worse. Coal could not leave the pits leading to nation-wide power cuts and food shortages. The Buchan line again

There is a train stuck somewhere in there. Even when snow was cleared, cuttings could quickly fill up again. This view is from an early 20th century postcard.   (GNSRA collection)

The bridge north of Mormond showing how much snow could accumulate. The track has been cleared but the number of footprints suggests that a lot of human effort was involved.   (GNSR collection)

suffered with a snowplough stuck in drifts at Newmachar and further blockages elsewhere.

January 1960 was another bad period when, among other problems, on the 20th a diesel multiple unit from Buchan to Aberdeen became completely snowed in near Newmachar.

Such incidents caused trouble for the railway and delay for the passengers, but little else. Not so on 12th March 1874 just south of Arnage when heavy snow led to a head-on collision that resulted in three deaths. On the previous two days driver John MacDonald and his fireman Alex Scott had worked their usual turn taking the 1.30am goods from Aberdeen to Keith and the 6.50am back. Because the snow was creating serious problems on the Buchan Line they were sent to assist trains as far as Udny and did not book off duty until 3pm the first day and 4pm the second. On

the 12th it was the same again only this time they worked to Auchnagatt, a part of the line unfamiliar to MacDonald. On his return, light engine, he should have complied with the time-table and stopped at Arnage to allow a northbound train to pass. For some reason he did not do so despite frantic efforts by the station staff to warn him. Scott was sure something was wrong but being in fear of his driver decided to consult the time-table before saying anything. As he did so he looked up and saw the approaching double headed train, jumped off and survived. The crew of the train engine did the same and also survived but the driver of the leading engine was killed at once while both his fireman and John MacDonald died the next day. While the Inspecting Officer laid the blame entirely on Driver MacDonald he made no reference to the, in our eyes, excessively long working hours required by the Company.

ROAD SERVICES AND OTHER LINES

Motor Bus Services

As has already been mentioned, the Great North recognised the value of motor buses in providing feeder services. The first service started in 1904 between Ballater and Braemar and the network developed over the next few years. Not all routes were successful and by the 1920s competition from other operators led to a gradual rundown of these services.

Three routes were operated in the Buchan area. The first introduced was from Udny to Methlick on 15th November 1904, only 6 months after that to Braemar. This served Pitmedden, Tarves and Keithfield. Between Keithfield and Methlick, various routes were followed, including via Haddo House. It does not appear to have been very successful as it ceased on 1st January 1907.

A much more successful route was that from Aberdeen to Newburgh, started on 1st September 1906. Two services were provided each way daily, plus a third on Wednesdays and Saturdays, taking 1½ hours for the journey for a fare of 1/9d, although day returns were available at 2/6d on Wednesdays (Aberdeen half-closing day) and Saturdays. This ceased on 1st March 1922, by which time there were competing services along the route. The third route was that from Fraserburgh to Rosehearty and New Aberdour which commenced 18th November 1912. Eight services were provided each way to Rosehearty, of which three continued to New Aberdour, taking just over an hour for the full distance. This service lasted until 11th July 1927.

A GNSR bus at Udny station, where it conveniently waited by the Down platform for passengers from Aberdeen. This was an early Milnes-Daimler bus, with limited capacity and rear access steps. The driver sat exposed at the front.   (K G Jones collection)

Lenabo Airship Base

During the Great War German U-boats were a constant danger to shipping and the Admiralty decided to build an airship station in the north-east to assist with protection against them. The favoured location was at Lenabo, about 2 miles south of Longside. At first materials for the base were unloaded at Mintlaw but this produced problems of its own. Not only was it some 5 miles away but the station yard was too small to cope, which resulted in stores being held as far away as Aberdeen waiting delivery. In the end extra sidings were authorised at Longside.

Even this did not ease the situation and in August 1915 the Railway Executive Committee enquired about the feasibility of providing a rail connection to the site, with the Great North acting as agents for its construction. The proposal had a chequered history. Only a month later the Admiralty decided it was too expensive, but clearly the idea had not been dropped as in August 1917 their Lordships asked for the work to be put in hand. All the same there seems to have been no great urgency as it was not until February 1918 that Messrs Tawse, Contractors, Aberdeen were awarded the contract for £23,015.13.9. Work was slow to start and it was not until October that the layout at Longside had been altered to allow access to the new line.

On leaving Longside the track turned sharply south-east to cross the South Ugie Water by means of a three span timber bridge, the only significant work on the route. From there it continued southwards climbing at about 1 in 60 and with minimal earthworks before turning west and entering the base.

There were three level crossings of public roads but gates were not considered necessary, a decision that led to a fatal accident in August 1923 when a train collided with a motor car, killing its driver

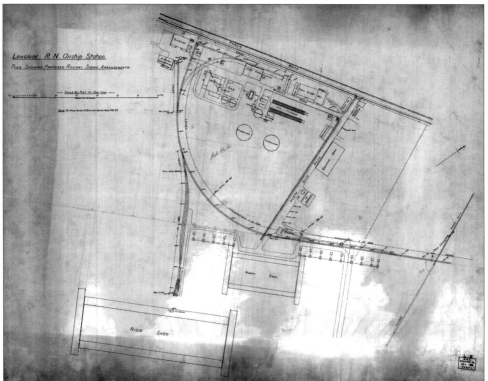

Plan of proposed sidings at Lenabo showing the line terminating parallel to the public road on the north side of the site. There is no record of what was actually installed.   (GNSRA collection)

and passenger.

Very little is known about the line or even who worked it – the Great North or the Admiralty. There is some conjecture that one of the ancient Great North locos built in 1856 and sold out of service in 1915 was used, but this is unlikely as the dates seem wrong. Equally there is some evidence that Messrs Tawse hired an engine from Dailuaine Distillery on Speyside but whether for use in construction or as agents for the Admiralty to work the trains is not clear.

The branch did not last long and closure came on 7th September 1923 when the connection at Longside was removed.

A few traces can be found to-day and there is an interpretation board to guide visitors. The foundations for the main buildings can be worked out, but forestation has covered all other signs.

Peterhead Harbour of Refuge Railway

The north-east coast of Aberdeenshire is very exposed in stormy weather so in 1884 the Admiralty started construction of a very large breakwater across Peterhead Bay to convert it into a secure all-weather harbour. The granite used in this work came from a quarry on Stirling Hill, about 2½ miles away, the quarry itself being worked by prisoners (convicts in those days) from the nearby prison which was opened in 1888. The quarry and breakwater were connected by a railway built to much higher standards than normally found on such a short industrial line.

The prisoners working the site were carried to and from the quarry in special vans, divided into several small compartments, with each van carrying 30-35 passengers. Trains ran twice daily in each direction. Five locomotives, all six-coupled tank engines built between 1889 and 1905

Stirling Hill Quarry. A group of prison workers are boarding the train to return to the prison. In the foreground, several loaded wagons are ready to be hauled down to the harbour. The locomotive is 'Edward VII'.   (GNSRA collection)

The body of one of the prison vans survived in a farmyard near St. Combs for many years. It was subsequently rescued and restored and now resides at Maud Museum.   (Keith Fenwick)

and named after members of the royal family, worked the line.

Uplifting the track along with dismantling and breaking up the rolling stock and locomotives began in 1950 and was spread over almost 8 years. To-day several sections of trackbed can be seen and a few coach bodies survive.

A separate line was built for the construction of the North Breakwater in 1911 and one of the tank engines was outstationed there.

Level crossings added to the cost of railway operation. There were three on the Buchan lines, each requiring the employment of a gatekeeper. After the passenger services were withdrawn, the gates were operated by train crew. This is Howe o'Buchan crossing not far from Peterhead with the guard doing the honours in June 1969.   (Keith Fenwick)

RUN DOWN

The railways in the north of Scotland resisted road competition for longer than many lines further south because of the longer hauls to and from centres in the south yielding greater revenue but by the mid-1950s road transport was steadily eating into the traffic. Parkhill closed in 1950 and Esslemont in 1952. Goods facilities were gradually withdrawn from the least used stations which then became unstaffed halts. Fish traffic generally transferred to road in the 1960s, but containerisation offered a means of keeping it on rail. Small containers were handled at Fraserburgh but the shift to larger ones meant that the traffic was carried there by road.

It must have come as little surprise therefore that the Beeching Report in 1963 proposed closure of all the Buchan lines to passenger traffic. Today's commuter traffic into Aberdeen was unknown then and buses took people much closer to their homes, ran more often and were cheaper. Peterhead and the St. Combs line closed on 3rd May 1965 but Fraserburgh retained its service until 4th October to enable substitute bus services to be arranged.

Goods facilities continued after passenger closure to Peterhead and Fraserburgh. The Crosse & Blackwell factory at Peterhead remained a rail customer but when that traffic was switched to Freightliner, the line from Maud was closed completely on 7th September 1970. The GNSRA was able to run a final farewell special along the line.

Traffic continued for several more years to Fraserburgh with Maud the only intermediate station to retain freight facilities. There was heavy traffic during the 1970s there as it was used as the railhead

The final train on the Peterhead line calls at Dyce on the return journey on 5th September 1970. Several special passenger trains also ran to Fraserburgh during the 1970s. (Norris Forrest)

The growth of the north sea oil industry in the 1970s gave rise to hopes that the railways would benefit. The only new traffic which came to the Buchan line was a flow of fabricated oil pipes conveyed on flat wagons and usually hauled by a couple of type 2 diesels. At Maud, the train had to be split into two to fit into the sidings.   (Norris Forrest)

for pipes manufactured at Invergordon for onward transport to St. Fergus. Reopening of the Peterhead line was mooted, but not progressed.

Throughout the 1970s, the line continued to operate with minimum maintenance. Speed was limited to 20mph. By 1979, the track had deteriorated so much that either money had to be spent or the line closed. And by then the pipeline traffic to Maud had ceased.

Funding for to keep the line could not be justified, so inevitably closure took place as from 8 October 1979. Apart from the last

train carrying a group of enthusiasts, the line went out with a whimper in contrast to the bang at its opening.

Since then, calls for the reopening of the line have been made several times, particularly the section as far as Ellon which could act as a railhead. The retention of the trackbed as described in the next chapter makes reasonably practical but even so the investment required will require a strong business case and has to compete with several other prospective line restorations further south.

Card tickets were usually issued for railtours in the 1970s.   (Keith Fenwick collection)

The Last Freight to Fraserburgh

Lewis McAllan described the last train for the Great North Review.

At 0645 hours on Friday, 5th October 1979, seven of our members assembled at the Shell in Aberdeen Joint station and, joined by an equal number from the Brechin Preservation Society and two pressmen, made our way to Platform 9, to board (by special arrangement with BR) the last scheduled freight train on the Buchan line, which, despite the usual representations in such circumstances, was to close on the following day. It was a grey, murky foggy morning and on the previous day the Aberdeen area had had the highest rainfall since records began - 3.6 inches in 24 hours!

In due course locomotive 27020 appeared with two bogie vehicles (for the parcels and us) and set back to collect ten Vanfits, one coal wagon (all loaded) and a rear brake van. At 07.12 we departed, with, in the cab, Driver Fred Smith, relief Driver Dick Anderson and Traction Inspector Bill Duncan. Guard Norman Thomson held the fort in the brake van. We also had with us, unofficially, the chief Passenger Trains Inspector for the Scottish Region, who proved equally adept at keeping an eye on freight trains. So we were well looked after.

With the Train Staff collected at Dyce signal box, we were in sole possession of all 40½ miles of the Buchan branch. Outside it was water, water everywhere - the swollen Don at Parkhill and lochs, great and small, in all the hollows of the land.

Now would come the climb to Newmachar, with a total load estimated by Inspector Duncan at 460 tonnes and on probably greasy rails. Someone produced a gradient profile showing 1 in 80/75 all the way to the Newmachar summit. "It looks like Annapurna", said one of the pressmen.

The last train stands at Fraserburgh, ready to depart for Aberdeen. The passenger station is on the left, behind the corrugated iron which formed its east wall; the track had been removed from it several years before. The train is standing at the main goods loading platform, once bustling with the loading of fish wagons.　　　　　　　　　　　　　　　　　　　　　　　　　　(Jonathan Dransart)

About half-way up we gradually came to a halt; the rails were indeed greasy. Thinking of all the other Buchan banks to come, we felt we would be out on a day, and not the expected half-day, trip. That was a fine feeling; we were ready for anything. With sand applied, Driver Smith managed to move forward inch by inch. Several times the process had to be repeated – stop, sand and away – until we were over the top. The journey between mileposts 10½ and 12 had taken 75 minutes. Kingseat Hospital had been in view, dimly through the haar, for so long that one began to wonder whether some obscure magnetic force was drawing us to it.

At Udny yard the sole remaining link with the past was the loading gauge, still standing lonely just outside the new housing estate. At Ellon the river Ythan looked more like the Mississippi. Charging on through the station, we heard the throttle opened for the next 1 in 75 bank to Arnage and this time there was no problem. After an unscheduled stop (reason unknown) near the point where the Auchnagatt Down home signal would once have stood, we pulled up in the Maud loop at 09.49.

The Vanfits and coal wagon were all for Maud and were detached. The engine and coaching vehicles ran forward into the station, of which the passengers made a thorough exploration and where a press photograph was taken of the whole company alongside the engine. Most of the Maud traffic was gravity shunted into the yard, under the eye of leading railman Jim Morrison, but in the end driver Smith had to set back and help.

At 10.23 Maud was left, with a load reduced to the two bogies and the brake van. At "Strichen Toon" the school classrooms were brightly lit against the gloom. A short blast from the horn and pupils looked up from their desks; a forest of little hands rose in a collective salutation.

Mormond summit was tackled in fine style, but where was Mormond Hill? With excess of modesty, she had completely covered herself, unable to bear the thought of looking for the last time at what she had seen so often for more than a century. Down through Lonmay, Rathen and Philorth and the loop outside Fraserburgh was reached at 10.50.

The engine came round and, after sending the brake van into a siding, propelled the two bogie vehicles into the main goods platform road, where we alighted. Until we arrived, the yard had been occupied by one coal wagon. The return journey commenced at 11.45. With the brake van left behind, we consisted of engine and two vehicles. The intention was to make a non-stop run to Dyce.

As we left there was the sound of detonators; at Strichen more waves from the schoolchildren; at Maud more detonators. With her limited load locomotive 27020 made short work of the gradients, and all went well through Brucklay and Esslemont and Logierieve and all those other places with names evocative of what had been. But suddenly on the descent from Newmachar there was an unexpected brake application. Someone looked out and cried, "Oh! There's a man with a red flag."

What had happened? Had the elements at last caught up with us? Had the Parkhill viaduct collapsed in the flood? Were we marooned, fated, Flying Dutchman-like, to travel for ever up and down the Buchan?

Not quite. True, there had been a small subsidence somewhere near Parkhill but we could proceed with caution.

We reached Dyce at 13.11 and after a few minutes waiting for the "road" we finally left the Buchan and drew up on platform 8 in Aberdeen at 13.29. We had enjoyed a smooth and comfortable run and a memorable outing.

So fare ye well, ye Mormond Braes: When again will you be seen from a train?

LIFE AFTER THE TRAINS

The final closure was particularly disappointing given that the development of the North Sea oil industry had given rise to hopes that it might be a saviour of the railway. A good deal of traffic, in the shape of large steel pipes for both sub-sea and overland pipelines, was indeed rail borne to Maud and Fraserburgh, but this was not enough to stave off the inevitable.

It was clear that the only realistic prospect of sustaining the large scale investment required to reopen the line in a form which could cope with heavy freight traffic was major industrial development in the area. The eventual decision in favour of pipelines to carry the North Sea oil and gas to the South effectively ended any real likelihood of a rebirth of the Buchan line.

The solum of the route was eventually purchased for a peppercorn by the Grampian Regional Council (itself now defunct) and converted over a number of years into a long distance footpath with information boards

and colourful mileposts illustrated here. This was formally opened on 12 June, 2000 as the Formartine and Buchan Way thus appropriately echoing the original name of the railway which it replaced. The Way affords splendid recreational opportunities to walkers, cyclists and horse riders through the heart of the Buchan countryside.

Starting at the north end of the car park at Dyce, it runs the whole length of the trackbed to

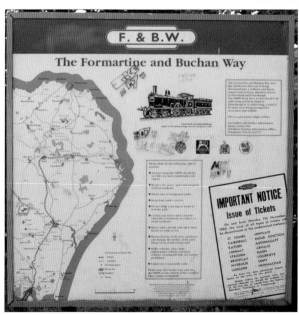

Users of the Formartine & Buchan Way are provided with information boards, such as the one on the left, and waymarkers in cast metal, such as the one above. Both these are at Parkhill, just north of the viaduct over the River Don. (Keith Fenwick)

both Peterhead and Fraserburgh, with a hard surface as far as Longside and from Inverugie into Peterhead. The other parts, including all of the Fraserburgh line, has a grassy surface. Some bridges have been removed. At the southern end at least the line still carries a few commuters, but nowadays on two wheels. For those who never knew it a walk brings to life all the stories about how difficult it was to operate trains in the face of a north-east blizzard.

Evidence of the railway itself does survive but in many cases it requires a keen eye and some background knowledge to detect. The station buildings which still stand have been converted to houses, except at Maud, with many of the goods yards used for more housing. Here and there can be seen a metal fence post or a gate and occasionally in the undergrowth the remains of a signal post cut off at ground level. A few lineside huts exist in various stages of disrepair but these are mainly of the standard British Railways 1950s type constructed of concrete panels. The most enduring and visible reminders of the railway are the bridges and viaducts constructed of Aberdeenshire granite of which the viaduct across the river Ythan at Ellon is perhaps the most striking.

The stations at Peterhead and Fraserburgh have vanished. The buildings at Fraserburgh were destroyed by fire in 1982. The old waiting room, ticket office and ancillary accommodation, which Grampian Regional Council bought with the station yard from British Rail, were completely burned out. After that the site was cleared and redeveloped, as was the site of the station at Peterhead, now occupied by Peterhead Academy and Community Centre.

At Maud the station buildings and platforms have survived. Much of the goods yard has been converted into a car park, with the rest of it set out as a wooded picnic area; the trees there are now well established. The station building was converted initially into business units for letting. Now it houses the Maud Railway Museum, described below.

You can read much more about the Formartine & Buchan Way in *Walking The Line* by Janet McLeman, published by the Association.

Maud Railway Museum

A small museum was established by the local authority in one of the business units at Maud in the 1995. Budget restrictions led to cutbacks in the opening of the museum and the involvement of volunteers in its operation. Eventually, operation was handed over entirely to volunteers and a charity Friends of Maud Railway Museum was set up.

The Friends now open the museum once or twice a month between April and October with free admission – but of course a donation is always welcome.

The volunteers have not only developed the displays but have enhanced the whole station site. The platforms have been cleared, as has some of the former goods yard where trees had taken over. The site of the turntable is easily found.

Several wagons are now on site and a short length of track has been laid. When the remaining business unit became available, it was secured for additional displays. A restored coach from Peterhead used by prisoners going to and from the quarry has found a home at Maud. Its occupants only had a short journey but the railways carried prisoners over much longer distances in similar conditions.

The museum has been popular with local people, many of whom remember the railway when it was still operating or even worked on the line. Their recollections have been recorded where possible to add to the aural history of the Great North. And many friendships have been born.

Details of open days can be found at friendsofmaud.org.uk and up-to-date news on facebook.com/MaudMuseum.

Two aerial views of Maud taken in January 2021. The one above is from the north end of the station with the Fraserburgh platform in the centre and the goods yard on the right. The lower view is from the south end looking north. The tracks of the two lines are just about discernible going to top left and right. The site of the turntable is prominent at the bottom of the photograph. Part of the goods yard provides a substantial car park for visitors to the museum and users of the Formartine & Buchan Way while the rest of it is in industrial use. It is remarkable to see how many bushes and trees have grown up; much effort has already been spent in clearing the area to the south of the buildings. While the whole site was neat and tidy when the Formartine & Buchan Way was opened, lack of maintenance since then has allowed unrestricted growth of bushes and trees. (Graeme Fisher)

An attractive display of paraphernalia greets visitors to the museum in 2019. All stations had platform barrows to carry luggage and parcels traffic to and from train. Inside, there is an operational model of the station. A future outside attraction will be a 5inch gauge miniature railway capable of carrying passengers. The museum is constantly expanding.   (Mike Cooper)

The restored Prison van at Maud. The original body is mounted on a wagon underframe. An unrestored body is shown on page 84.   (Keith Jones)

APPENDIX: OPENING AND CLOSING DATES

	Name	Dist	Opened	Closed		Notes
				Passenger	Goods	
Dyce to Peterhead	Dyce	0				
	Parkhill	1¼	18.7.1861	3.4.1950	7.8.1961	
	Newmachar	5¼	18.7.1861	4.10.1965	23.3.1964	
	Udny	8¼	18.7.1861	4.10.1965	28.3.1966	
	Logierieve	10	18.7.1861	4.10.1965	7.11.1960	1
	Esslemont	11½	18.7.1961	15.9.1952	15.9.1952	
	Ellon	13¼	18.7.1861	4.10.1965	11.9.1967	
	Arnage	16¾	18.7.1861	4.10.1965	23.3.1964	
	Auchnagatt	20½	18.7.1861	4.10.1965	28.3.1966	
	Maud Junction	24½	18.7.1861	4.10.1965	8.10.1979	2
	Abbey of Deer	27¼				3
	Mintlaw	29	18.7.1861	4.10.1965	19.6.1967	4
	Longside	32	3.7.1862	3.5.1965	23.3.1964	5
	Newseat	34½	3.7.1862	3.5.1965	N/A	
	Inverugie	35¾	3.7.1862	3.5.1965	7.11.1960	
	Peterhead	38	3.7.1862	3.5.1965	7.9.1970	
	Peterhead Harbour	39	9.8.1865	N/A	by 1939	
Fraserburgh Section	Maud	0				
	Brucklay	1¾	24.4.1865	4.10.1965	28.3.1966	
	Strichen	5¾	24.4.1865	4.10.1965	19.6.1967	
	Mormond	8¼	24.4.1865	4.10.1965	1.6.1940	
	Lonmay	10¾	24.4.1865	4.10.1965	23.3.1964	
	Rathen	13¼	24.4.1865	4.10.1965	7.11.1960	
	Philorth	14½	24.4.1865	4.10.1965		6
	Tool Works	15¾	6.2.1905	N/A		
	Fraserburgh	16	24.4.1865	4.10.1965	8.10.1979	
Cruden Section	Ellon	0				
	Auchmacoy	3¼	2.8.1897	31.10.1932	7.11.1945	
	Pitlurg	5½	2.8.1897	31.10.1932	7.11.1945	
	Hatton	8¼	2.8.1897	31.10.1932	7.11.1945	
	Cruden Bay	10¼	2.8.1897	31.10.1932	7.11.1945	
	Brick & Tile Wks	11	22.8.1902	N/A		
	Bullers O'Buchan	12	1899	31.10.1932	N/A	
	Longhaven	13½	2.8.1897	31.10.1932	7.11.1945	
	Boddam	15¼	2.8.1897	31.10.1932	7.11.1945	
St. Combs branch	Fraserburgh	0				
	Kirkton Bridge Halt	1	1904	3.5.1965	N/A	
	Philorth Bridge Halt	2	1.7.1903	3.5.1965	N/A	
	Cairnbulg	3½	1.7.1903	3.5.1965	7.11.1960	7
	St. Combs	5	1.7.1903	3.5.1965	7.11.1960	

Notes
1 Called Newburgh Road from opening for at least 3 months.
2 Called Brucklay from opening until 24.4.1865, then New Maud until 30.12.1867.
3 Special platform for pilgrimages mentioned in various publications, 1932 to 1947.
4 Called Old Deer & Mintlaw until 1.9.1867
5 Branch from Longside to Royal Naval Airship Station Lenabo, 2 miles. Temporary connection brought into use 2.12.1918. Connection removed 7 September 1923.
6 Private station for Lord Saltoun until 9.6.1926.
7 Called Inverallochy until 3.8.1903.

BIBLIOGRAPHY

Collins Encyclopedia of Scotland, J & J Kaye,
Cruden Bay Hotel and Tramway, GNSRA.
Earl of Aberdeen's Railway, David Fasken, GNSRA
Great North of Scotland Railway, David Ross, Stenlake Publishing.
Great North of Scotland Railway, H A Vallance, House of Lochar.
Great North of Scotland Railway Locomotives, Hugh Gordon, Irwell Press.
History of the Great North of Scotland Railway, Sir Malcolm Barclay-Harvey, Ian Allan.
Peterhead Train, A G Murdoch.
Story and Tales of the Buchan Railway, Alan Sangster, Oxford Publishing Co.
Walking the Line, A Curious Walker's Guide to the Formartine & Buchan Walkway, Janet McLeman, GNSRA

Great North *Review*
Peterhead Sentinel
Formartine & Buchan Railway Minute Books
GNSR Minute Books
BR Papers

The Transport Treasury : many of the photographs in this book were taken by Sandy Murdoch and Norris Forrest, whose collections were donated to the GNSRA. A selection of their photographs is now available commercially from The Transport Treasury, along with a large range of other railway photographs from all parts of Great Britain. See www. transporttreasury.co.uk/ for full lists and how to order prints.

A group of permanent way workers about to set of on a hand-propelled trolly. They carried the single line token to ensure that no train came along while they were at work, which could include replacing worn rails or fishplates.   (Sandy Murdoch/GNSRA)

Walking the Line : A Curious Walker's Guide to the Formartine and Buchan Way, by Janet M McLeman. Published by the GNSRA. 112pp, 112 colour and 16 black and white illustrations, B5. ISBN 978 0902343 28 3. £9.90.

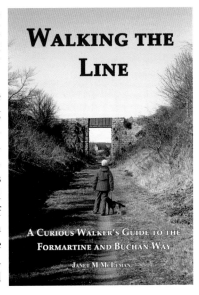

The Formartine and Buchan Way is a long distance footpath on the disused railway line linking the fishing ports of Fraserburgh and Peterhead with Aberdeen. It traverses the heartlands of rural Aberdeenshire, a land of prehistoric monuments, medieval castles, ruined churches and abbeys, scenes of ferocious religious conflicts, Jacobite strongholds, abandoned mills, the planned villages and elegant mansions of the improving lairds and the only hill carvings in Scotland. A valuable wild life corridor, the Formartine and Buchan Way is now a rich habitat for wild flowers, birds and mammals, many of which are endangered by modern farming methods used elsewhere.

This book describes what can be seen on and near the Way. You will be surprised how interesting a walk can be and just how much there is to find. This book will be of interest to those who recall the days before closure of the line as well as to those who enjoy its recreational facilities.

Order through www.gnsra.org.uk.

Great North of Scotland Railway Association

Founded 1964

The Association caters for all those interested in the history of the Great North of Scotland Railway and its constituent companies, as well as the lines during the LNER, British Railways and post-privatisation periods. The Association promotes the study and collection of information, documents and illustrations relating to all aspects of the North East's railways. It also facilitates and co-ordinates members' research and provides information for modellers.

Members receive a quarterly *Review* containing articles, photographs, drawings and news of the railway, both historical and current. The Association has produced a comprehensive range of books and technical papers covering aspects of the railway in great detail. Members have access to an extensive photographic and drawing archive. Members receive a discount on Association publications. Meetings and excursions are regularly organised.

For further information, please look at the Association's website

www.gnsra.org.uk

Cuttings in the relatively flat ground of the Buchan could easily fill up with snow, whipped up by winds from the north. Railwaymen fought year after year to keep the line open. This view from about 1960 shows a diesel multiple unit stuck near Newmachar as a stop notorious for blockages. Even if a snowplough was available, shovels were needed to clear the snow close to the train. (Graham Maxtone collection)